GO FISHING FOR

TROUT

GRAEME PULLEN

The Oxford Illustrated Press

The Oxford Illustrated Press

© 1989 Graeme Pullen

ISBN 0 946609 80 2

Published by:
The Oxford Illustrated Press Limited, Haynes Publishing Group,
Sparkford, Nr Yeovil, Somerset BA22 7JJ, England.

Haynes Publications Inc., 861 Lawrence Drive, Newbury Park, California
91320, USA.

Printed in England by:
J.H. Haynes & Co Limited, Sparkford, Nr Yeovil, Somerset.

British Library Cataloguing in Publication Data
Pullen, Graeme
    Go fishing for trout.
    1. Salmon & trout. Angling – Manuals
    I. Title
    799.1'755
    ISBN 0-94660-980-2

Library of Congress Catalog Card Number
    89–80214

Contents

Acknowledgements

I would like to thank Michael Leech of the International Game Fish Association, Florida, USA, for the use of his lake trout photo and supplying the world record listings, and also Airflo Lines for their assistance with fly line detail and Mr. Alan Bramley of Partridge of Redditch for his guide to trout fishing hooks.

Dedication

To Hilary, for letting me go fishing
so often . . . It is *work* after all!

Introduction

The world of trout fishing has been revolutionised over the last twenty years. The 1970s and 1980s saw the rainbow assert itself as our premier still-water game fish, and it holds that position not so much from popular demand, as from the fact that it is the fastest-growing species of trout. Trout have been around for possibly millions of years, evolving into primarily a cold-water species, and sought after for food by our ancestors. No one species has had such a following among fishermen, or had so much written about its habitat, habits and the techniques for its capture.

This book aims to give you a complete picture of how the sport for this fish has increased, and some of the better ways to catch it. As a youngster I remember reading of the mystique surrounding the stalking and capture of a 1-lb fish from a difficult position—the tenacity of its fight, its heart-stopping acrobatics as it tried to throw the hook, and of course, the tackle and methods used. There is enough for several books on the subject. The 'best' method to catch a trout is often the only method a particular writer has had any success with!

I have caught trout on worms, maggots, spinners, plugs, dry flies, lures, nymphs, sweetcorn, sugar puffs, currant cake, bread, crust and marshmallows! I have fished them in lakes and streams, from the mountain streams of the Atlantic island of Madeira, to a Hampshire chalk stream and a wind-swept reservoir in the border country of Scotland, from a quiet, peat-tainted river in Ireland to serene lakes in the unmatched splendour of the Apache White Mountains of Arizona, and the Drakensberg mountains and rivers of South Africa. Am I then an expert on the subject? I would say not, for with trout fishing there is no such thing as an expert, merely those who have a little more understanding and experience of fishing for them. Some people may like to call themselves 'experts' on trout, but there is no one person who knows all there is to know. Every time you go fishing you should learn something from the trip, even if it's that you hate trout, and will never go again!

Our original trout was the brown trout, a speckled gold-flanked beauty that was protected and revered by the few that had either the position or the finance, or both, to pursue them in their natural environment. Then along came the 'rebel', a species called the rainbow that was alleged to have superior fighting qualities, came avidly to the fly or bait, and leapt considerably on hooking. It was a fast grower, and such qualities quickly became apparent to the fish farmers. They could pump the same amount of commercially made protein feed into a rainbow, and yet get a fish bigger than the browns. The rainbow was in, and the poor old brown was on its way out. With cheaper fast-growing fish came the drop in price that brought the species within the pocket of all. Even the ordinary working man could afford a day after the trout, where previously access to trout waters was limited, syndicated, or refused. Those who had revered the traditional English brown trout fishing closed ranks, and bemoaned the fact that the rainbow had taken over. Many others treated this newcomer with delight.

I loved catching rainbows, but now, a few years on, I have come to understand why those men treated the traditional British brownie as their god. He is naturalised, as British as you or me, and deserves a fate better than to run second best to the rainbow just because he grows a bit more slowly. Now there are those on the trout farms who undertake the worrying task of pushing brown trout through the system, as more anglers tire of catching gullible rainbows, and go back to the majestic brown. When you catch a truly wild fish, laid as an egg in some remote stream, which has fought its way against the current and predators, and our own pollution, to grow up to a respectable size, then you will hook a fish that puts up a struggle second to none. It's still 'just' a trout, but it is British, and deserves to be treated with a little respect. It is something of a rarity, so if you are fortunate enough to catch a truly 'wild' fish it's better to put it back alive. It would probably taste good, but being in the minority of the piscine population, give it a second chance. For next time you throw a fly or lure at it, that fish will be more cautious about accepting your offering. If you can tempt it another day, then you really can call yourself a trout fisherman.

About the Species

There are many subspecies of trout and char. For a time, when fish farming in the UK was experimenting with different strains, we had brook trout, tigers, cheetahs and shasta. Presumably the novelty wore off, for few of these species are taken nowadays. Public demand, coupled with the cost of production and high mortality rates, can mean the demise of a new species within a year.

Of all the freshwater species I have ever fished for and caught, the rainbow trout is simply the most greedy, stupid fish of all. They will, in their wild state, pounce upon anything with a predatory instinct that makes pike and zander seem like vegetarians. In my opinion, the only reason that fly fishing was devised for them was because they were so easy to catch, they had to be protected, by a cumbersome rod with a short butt, and a reel that barely succeeds in playing the fish out, and can only really be called a line storage device. Then we come to the subject of flies. Numerous books have been written on the subject of entomology, and the care with which a trout sips down a tiny insect. But give the trout the choice between a blue-winged olive and a bunch of worms, and I'll put my money on it taking the worms!

It must be said, however, that the art of casting with a fly line can be pleasurable, even if you catch nothing, and it was after all, devised as a way of presenting something that weighs nothing to a waiting fish. Fly fishing itself can be a pleasing way of taking trout, but don't be fooled into thinking it is the only or even the best way to take them. You would be forgiven for thinking that fly fishing is the be-all and end-all of trout fishing. I have travelled to a few countries in the world and there are more than a few ways to catch fish!

Profile of a big Brook trout. This species responds best in cold conditions and becomes lethargic in many of the south's warmer waters.

Where to Fish Trout

Weir Pools

The British Isles plays host to some superb big brown trout waters, where the fish have grown on from the egg, and where it is still possible to take monster fish without resorting to a fish farm specimen. The river Thames, for instance, still has some brown trout in it, mostly in weir pools, but they only get fished for a couple of times a year, mainly by the dyed-in-the-wool river brownie enthusiast. Fishing in the weir pools above Berkshire and around Pangbourne I have seen tremendous browns turn over in the fast water, or take some fry on the shallows. Some of them may run to double figures, and I have landed them myself to just under 4 lb.

To see such a beautiful wild fish leaping and crashing around will start your heart thumping, but you need to fish for them with fairly specialised techniques. For these wild weir pool browns I would say forget the fly gear. These fish have lived in fast water and have had to build up strength on beetles, terrestrial wash-ins via the weir sill, and of course the millions of coarse fish fry that abound in the spring and summer months. The best area is directly to the side of the main weir pool chute, as you must remember they favour areas of highly oxygenated water, while remaining on station in the current waiting for anything that drifts past their noses. All weir pools have this main chute, but the water underneath, near the gravel bed, and slightly to the side will be much slower than the surface water.

The best time of year will be spring and summer, the best baits either worms or minnows. You may wonder why I don't suggest lures, spinners or plugs. A lot of these weir pools get fished for pike by the coarse fishermen who throw plugs and lures of all descriptions across the pool. The browns don't get large by being stupid, and they have a memory retention far greater than the gullible rainbow. They will occasionally follow a lure out of curiosity, but they rarely take it. The normal coarse fish baits of maggots and bread are ignored, although I once took a 3 lb 9-oz wild brown on swimfeeder and maggots intended for bream. These fish are looking for small fry and the minnow should be fished without any form of float or bite detection device that might put them off. You will have to learn the art of freelining, which allows your offering to be fished with either its own body weight, or with just a single swan shot to get down through the current. Keep that swan shot at least two feet from the minnow, otherwise you may get a dropped run. Unlike pike and perch, a brown is unlikely to come back a second time, as they tend to frighten easily. You can use a 5-lb line straight through to a size 8 freshwater hook, and either fish the minnow live, which is by far the better way, or fish it dead.

You should be aware that if you are casting right up to the edge of a weir sill—which is the best place in my opinion, as the water has a high oxygen content, and there is a more comfortable flow for a predator to rest in—a live minnow can swim right up under the sill out of harm's way. So if you use live bait, cast it several feet down-current from the weir sill, so that it is exposed in open water. If you livebait with minnows, take a tip and, with 3-lb line, whip a smaller size 16 hook to the bend of the size 8. This will be used to liphook the minnow through the top lip only, causing minimal bait damage, and letting him stay more active.

If you deadbait with one however, you can use just the big size 8 and hook him with this through both lips, so his mouth stays shut. The deadbait can be fished as close as you want to weir sills or overhanging branches, as you are the one directing its movements. Once cast out, you should let it sink slowly, then twitch it back across the current, watching the slack formed by the bow in the line. If you don't feel the take on the rod top, you should watch for a tug in the

The Sea Trout. A sea run Brown trout grows to a good size in the wild because of the rich feeding available. Shrimps and other small fish are rich in protein, enabling it to return to the rivers many pounds heavier each season. This wild Sea Trout of over 10 lb was caught by an angler using swimfeeder and maggots from the Severals Fishery of the Hampshire Avon at Ringwood. Note the perfect proportions of this fish, possibly the most powerful of all trout species, certainly in British waters.

slack line. Be prepared to give line immediately, so the brown can get the bait inside his mouth. Close the bail arm and strike firmly. It is as simple as that. You are going to catch some good perch using this method, and certainly will at some time or other become acquainted with pike. Treat each fish hooked with respect, because you never know when a large brown is going to latch onto your minnow.

In Victorian times when there were a lot more brown trout in the Thames, the anglers would use something called drop-minnow tackle. This was two hooks, small trebles, and a tiny cone-shaped lead with a spike to slot down the throat of the minnow. The lead would take the minnow straight to the bottom, where it was bounced in sink-and-draw fashion down the current. Needless to say with a pair of tiny trebles its hooking efficiency was high, but I think a competent modern angler could do just as well with a single hook.

With worms, you need a couple of big lobworms on the same size hook. You can freeline them as for the minnows, or you can make up a running leger and fish them in the fast current at the tail of the main weir run. Make sure you keep your rod up high, both to minimise water pressure on the line, and to be able to give some slack to a taking fish. Brown trout can take a bunch of lobworms down the back of their throat with frightening rapidity, but again, if you want fish of over 3 lb, I would give them a second or two before striking. To give some freedom of movement to the worms, I fish them on a tail at least four feet long. That means stopping the running leger at least four feet from the hook. The first indication of a bite is when the tip jumps round, and by holding the rod all the time, you can 'give slack' to a taking fish immediately.

In Arkansas on a famous river below a reservoir I fished with a professional trout guide. The water run-off from the base of the dam was very, very cold, and trout thrived in it. There was little or no insect life due to this low temperature, but the further I travelled down river, the more the temperature rose. Here and there were small blooms of weed, and it was opposite these weedbeds that we anchored the boat. Wherever there was weed there would be food, and the trout circled the weedbeds looking for offerings. They took best if the worm was cast right on top of the weed. Unfortunately the worm wriggled its way out of sight into the weed. The guide injected air into the worm using a hypodermic syringe, and then counterbalanced this by adding shot until the bait was perfectly balanced and slow sinking. Then it would drift down and rest on top of the weedbed. I took several wild rainbows using this method, and it is something you can use in rivers that are slow, or have an abundance of weed in them.

Worming really is a bit of an art, and it must surely be the most basic method of all fishing. You go into the garden, dig up some worms and put the 'Gone Fishin' ' sign on the office door!

Small Streams

You have to adapt your technique a little when you venture onto small streams and brooks. Here the water will be much more shallow, faster flowing, and the wild trout will be smaller. They still represent good sport though, and can be taken on a variety of methods and baits, especially worms. A good rig from yesteryear was called Stewart tackle. It consisted of three single hooks fixed an inch apart on the line, to hold the worm out straight by nicking it in the tail, centre and head. It was a good way to hold them, but possibly frowned on by most angling clubs today. There is no reason why you shouldn't have the same hooking capacity using just a single hook, and just nick them near the head a couple of times. When you cast them out, the body invariably straightens and the flow will hold them straight. All you have to do is to let the trout have the worm a second or two longer, to allow them sufficient time to get it well inside their mouth.

Apart from times of falling water after a flood, in which the worm is deadly, the next best time to use worms is in high summer when low water conditions make trout lie unperturbed in the current. You will still have to look for something of a feature in the water—the inside of a bend, a boulder, a log sticking out from the bank, overhanging branches trailing in the current, the rough water of tiny rapids. You may be able to spot the fish visually. If you can do this you can position yourself well upsteam, and freeline the worm down, ensuring that it flows constantly down the current, at an even rate. I cannot stress too strongly the importance of not letting it stop in fits and jerks. Apart from a live or injured fish, most food items washed down to a waiting trout do so at an even pace. You must conform to what they are used to seeing.

If the approach is visual, you may actually see the trout swing out and gulp down the worm. Don't strike immediately, pause a second or so, drop the reel in gear and strike, making sure there are no overhead branches or bushes to obstruct the strike. If the water is clear, but you can't quite make out the shape of the fish, you must fish in very close contact with the worm. Should the depth be four feet or less, degrease the end of the line for the first three feet from the

The author fishes a wet fly downstream using a leaded nymph. Wet fly downstream is far more successful due to the current straightening out any curves in the line, thus putting the angler in instant contact with a taking fish. In addition, a fly coming against the current seems to make the trout more aggressive, and gives a better take.

hook using washing up liquid, then grease the remaining six feet from there, up the line, using mucilin. If the worm is a brandling or redworm weighted with just a bb shot, you should be able to watch the line where it enters the surface film for any signs of a bite when it passes by the feature. Pause, give the fish time to take the worm, then strike.

If the stream is overgrown you may have to get in the water with waders, and work your way carefully down to the feature, moving your feet carefully so as to disturb the bottom as little as possible. Your profile will be lower so the trout is unlikely to see you so early.

The author fishes the upstream nymph on his own stretch of Hampshire river. In order to maintain contact with the fly you must constantly retrieve at a speed not likely to disturb the natural momentum of the fly, but one that keeps you in direct contact with it. Always watch the tip of the leader and strike as soon as it pauses.

What he will detect though is vibration, so exercise care in approaching. Against this, you have to take into account that the lower you are to the water surface, the less you will be able to see through the water. Don't work your way down the centre of the stream. Keep in towards one bank or the other, trying to get on the opposite side of any feature you think might hold a fish. Trout are never spread all over the bottom of the river bed. They will stay in areas where the food items come readily to them, or which may offer them a bit of security from predators.

In clear water, if you are bank fishing, try to avoid casting directly on top of the fish. Your cast, when it lands, can be adjusted to ensure it runs down directly to the fish, preferably with your worm as the first thing it sees. Any line that falls across its vision can frighten it, so place the cast carefully. With worm fishing, you can get right in amongst the 'jungly' bits of river that the fly fisherman cannot reach, and very often this is the place the better fish in the stream lie.

Never work your way downriver to the bottom end of the beat or section you have chosen. You will find it almost impossible to get the fishing position you need without frightening the fish. This is especially true of shallow chalk streams. Start at the bottom end of the beat and walk slowly up until you spot the fish lying on station. Then walk across the river in a wide circle, and come in twenty yards upstream, having made a mental note where the trout lies in relation to a piece of bankside vegetation. Come in on a low crouch, and either keep low on the bank, or get in the stream with waders before you cast. You can certainly see plenty of trout when you frighten them, but they may not settle down until the following day, and that's too late!

This was illustrated to me on one of the many 'Fishtrek' trips I have had, with Paul Harris, the angling advisor to the Irish Tourist Board. We had stopped the van on a bridge over a small feeder stream between two loughs. Some of our group were going on elsewhere, two of them wanted to go pike fishing on the lough, and a boat had been moored on the river for them. As I stood on the bridge and watched them getting in the boat, a monster brown rocketed upstream, thoroughly frightened by all the noise and activity. I shouted to the others, who couldn't believe that I had seen what appeared to be a 6-lb wild brown in what they thought was a drainage ditch. Fortunately, it shot back downstream, turned round and finally disappeared upstream for good, this time giving everybody a good look.

Where there's one there must be more, so next day Paul and I left the party to their own devices and found ourselves on the bridge. Our first mistake was to walk along the high bank between the trees, peering into the water to see if there was more than one fish. We trudged a good way before we frightened one, and it bolted downstream in traditional fashion. We decided to start at the lower end and work upstream! It was half a mile before Paul spotted the first wild brown, perfectly camouflaged against the peat-stained Irish stones. Doubtless we had missed several, but this one was lying a third of the way across the stream directly underneath an overhanging branch, trailing spring flood debris from its branches. All we could see was the white of its jaw, slowly opening and closing. I circled away from the bank, while Paul lay on his stomach to direct operations and watch the trout's reaction. I came into the water about twenty yards upsteam of the trout, just on the edge with a bush to my back so he couldn't see me. There was no way I could cast, and the shot I had on the line made the worm wedge in the stones before it reached the trout's position.

I took off the shot, and using just the weight of the worm, swung it out to the far bank. I let the current take hold, and line flipped from the reel as the worm went on its way. About five yards in front of the trout I stopped it, and lifted the rod top to bring the worm to the surface so that Paul could see its positioning. The first cast was too far left, then too far right. Finally I got it right, and Paul said in a loud whisper, 'That's good. It's right on line.' When I judged the worm to be near the overhanging tree branch I could resist it no longer. 'What's he doing?' There was a pause, then Paul whispered back 'I can't see your worm any more, but the trout's mouth is snapping away like mad.' I knew what that was, so tightened down and struck. The shouts of glee when that brown came out could have been heard on the next lough. Its gold flank shimmered in the sunlight as it bounced out of the water like a red speckled ball. I played it and Paul met me on the bank as we admired the colours and shape of this truly wild fish. It was a couple of pounds, and certainly worth keeping, but even though the others might mock us, we decided to release it. With a kick of its tail it had gone. Although we scoured every nook and cranny of the walk back, we could see no sign of the previous day's 6-lb brown. At least we knew they could be caught, even though two of us had to take part in its downfall.

Just as we neared the stone bridge, I saw another brown, lying directly in the shade on the downstream side of the bridge. It was bigger, but not as big as 6 lb. There was no way I dared cast to it from this close, so we adopted the same tactics. Paul would act as 'spotter', while I climbed up, crossed the road, and waded in on the upstream side of the bridge. Again, it took several casts to get the right line and pace for the worm, and then the worm snagged on stones about five feet short of the trout! What should I do? If I retrieved I might frighten it, but surely it couldn't see the worm on the stones?

'What are you doing,' whispered Paul, 'I can't see the worm.' I replied that it was stuck, and started to gently tweak it from the stones.

'I can't see the trout,' said Paul, 'he must have gone.' As I tugged at the worm, something started tugging back. He must have it!

'I think he's got it, Paul,' I yelled.

'But I can't see the trout, and now I can't see the bloody worm,' he said.

'I know, it's inside the trout.'

With this, I struck and the water under the bridge erupted as the brown took off like a greyhound. I couldn't follow it under the bridge without risking a soaking, so applied as much pressure as I dared. That only antagonised the fish, which bolted up past me and let me put sidestrain on. By now Paul had scrambled up the bridge and was running for the cameras.

The fish was all of $3\frac{1}{2}$ lb, maybe 4, and had an iridescent golden sheen to it. After holding it gently out of the water for photographs I unhooked and returned it. It was thoroughly exhausted and swam off quietly to regain its strength. From up on the bridge we could vaguely make out its shape, in just three feet of clean water, so good was its camouflage.

You might think things like this only happen in Ireland, but of course many English streams have wild browns in them as well, it's just that nobody fishes for them as a separate species.

Where to Fish Trout

Fast Waters

Now let's look at the large fast waters with rapids. Rapids generally mean shallow water, and where a body of water increases in speed and is broken there will be a higher oxygen content. That spells trout, and on these rapids, a more effective way than fishing with a worm is with a small mepps spinner. But if you cast a spinner down a fast current and attempt to bring it back on the retrieve, you find the blades of the spinner bite the water, making it run near the surface. That's no good, because the blades are revolving too fast in relation to the spinner's speed. It must after all, be a moving food item, not just a stationary revolving piece of metal. For this reason you need to make your cast directly across the stream flow, or better still slightly upcurrent. That not only allows the spinner to drop down deeper in the water, but it allows its blades to work more efficiently through the water. Many small trout will fall for this technique, and also the occasional big fish, at first and last light. The spinner obviously unlocks that predatory instinct present in all trout, so you would think the minnow baits would work. But for some reason they don't, although the odd fish comes out on them. I can only assume that wide, fast-flowing rivers aren't the natural habitat of minnows and the trout don't come to expect them as a regular part of their diet.

Lochs and Reservoirs

Trout live very well in large bodies of water like lochs and reservoirs. In fact with the biggest of the predatory browns, this is a favoured habitat. There are three methods worth mentioning here. In America and many other countries, you can go fishing for rainbows using any method, rather than being restricted to fly only. Quite the best bait I have known for stillwater rainbows is sweetcorn. This drives them completely mad, but the trick lies in firing out several grains of sweetcorn regularly so there is a constant flow of them through the water. Whether the golden colour sends them scatty I don't know, but if you want the most takes, leger a couple of grains of sweetcorn

Go Fishing for Trout

Possibly the most productive area on many of our larger reservoirs. A good breeze blowing on the dam wall will confine the trout and in addition, the angler in this boat is fishing a sinking line near the draw-off from the main valve tower. A prime area for big Browns.

on the bottom. Much of the loose feed you threw in will be down on the bottom, and while many anglers feel that rainbows only feed in the surface layers, you will get more takes 'down on the deck'! Trout, as I have said, are opportunist feeders and will be wherever the food is. To isolate your grains of sweetcorn from the rest you need them suspended off the bottom. You should do this without the use of a float which would make the line hang down through the water, and

Where to Fish Trout

Above: Britain offers good semi-wild trout in many of the reservoirs and they provide sport for the angler who likes to fish either bank or boat.

Right: While fly fishing will bring the odd big wild brownie like this one, many more go undisturbed simply because although the angler can get a lead core fly line down to their depth, he can only fish up and down, not laterally through the water at any sort of depth.

the trout might see it. Add a small marshmallow to the point of the hook which is buoyant and keeps the corn up off the bottom. A lot of American anglers believe it is the marshmallow that the trout want and I think this could well be true. Of course most of the British waters hold a fly-only restriction, but if you ever get to some of the 'any method' venues, give corn and marshmallow a try.

For big browns in large bodies of open water, whether reservoirs in England, lochs in Scotland or loughs in Ireland, I suggest you use the same method—deep-water trolling. I was first introduced to this technique, not in the UK where most people have never even heard of it, but in the state of Utah, where the world famous Flaming Gorge reservoir lies. This enormous body of water has produced some incredible fish, including browns to over 33 lb, lake trout to 34 lb and rainbows (wild) to 27 lb.

After going on a skiing promotion outside Salt Lake City, you can imagine that it wasn't long before my wife Hilary and I found ourselves driving up past the grazing elk of the forests towards the border with Wyoming! It's a remote place, even a bit eerie, much like Dungeness beach on a wild winter night, but the lodge where the guides worked from was littered with mounts of huge lake trout and browns. Here they specialise in downrigger trolling, which means you fish with either a big plug made by Rapala, or a heavy metal spoon which is clipped via a release clip to a lead downrigger ball. You basically run your lure back twenty or thirty yards, then put the line into an outrigger clip. The lead ball is housed near the clip, and the whole lot is lowered on an electronic winch down to whatever depth you want to run the lure at—ten feet, fifty feet, even a hundred feet. When a fish grabs the lure, the pull breaks the outrigger clip and you are free to play the fish in the normal fashion. You can run a couple of fish locators and echo sounders at the same time, thus getting a picture of what the bottom is like under the hull of the boat, then raising the downrigger ball or lowering it according to ledges, bait shoals, or with a sophisticated unit, even the individual fish.

Flaming Gorge is stocked with rainbows by the relevant Fisheries Departments, and the predators have to locate a food fish, usually threadfin shad, which is the diet that pushes them to such enormous weights in the wild. Talking to one of the guides as we trolled with a

The trout fisherman in America looks to the latest equipment to assist him in finding monster trout. Sounders like this Sonic Wave 660S model are capable of marking bottom contours, shoals of baitfish and even individual predators like the large Browns and Lake trout.

pair of downriggers, I learned that many of the really big lake trout, and browns, fed not on the shad, but on the rainbows that were stocked in the first place! All the guides I spoke to had caught lake trout up to and over 30 lb that had 2-lb or 3-lb rainbows inside them! Trolling one of these could present problems! However it serves to illustrate just how predatory trout can be.

There were two schools of thought concerning the location of the big browns and lake trout. Some guides relied entirely on locating the shoals of smaller fish, and ran the Rapala lures, via the downriggers, to slightly below and to the side of the baitfish. This way they would optimise the strike period, rather than trolling lures blindly around a

Having established what depth either the trout or their baitfish are feeding at, the line is clipped to a downrigger ball or paravane weight to run the lure down as deep as 100ft. Here you can see the traditional downrigger in the shape of the circular ball, and the aero, or water dynamic shape of the Riviera downrigger weight.

Having clipped the lure into the downrigger system and run the line to the predetermined depth, the rod is wound over tight against the clip, so the second a strike occurs, the amount of slack taken by the trout is minimal. The lure and downrigger can be raised and lowered electronically to fish the exact contours of any underwater structure.

big reservoir. Even with such sophistication as the Sonic Wave cathode ray tube colour readouts, you can still 'hook fish you don't see, and see fish you don't hook'.

The reservoir specifications of Flaming Gorge makes interesting reading compared to our 'large' waters like Rutland and Grafham. It's 90 miles long, and is full of canyons. It's fed by the Green River in the north which has its beginnings above Wyoming and Montana, wending its way southward into the Colorado system. It was dammed and flooded in 1964–65, and in 1966 the water started to back up.

The second method for taking these super-size trout is deep jigging. This is a method used in colder weather, when the fish are lying very deep, and are loath to move very far for a meal. With depths up to 300 feet you can see that location of either baitfish or trout with electronic equipment is imperative.

The third method is flatfishing. This is slow trolling using a wire line and a curved, banana-shaped flat plug that judders its chin along the bottom. This digging motion is designed to represent a crayfish, and while it is used in shallower water, you still look to the sounder to give you information. Instead of looking for a shoal of baitfish, the angler using flatfish needs a high-tech sounder that shows the lake trout itself, lying on the bottom. Having fished this method as well, I can testify that you *can* see the shape of the fish on the bottom.

The best depth to cover all these species of monster trout is between 40 and 80 feet and the best month is October when the mackinaw, or big lake trout move into shallower depths to spawn. In winter, from December to April, this enormous body of water freezes over, but even then the dedicated big trout angler gears up to his power-sled, and drives across the ice with his sounder running, as the waves can still travel through ice to pick up fish marks below. They then stop the sled, jump out and using a special circular cutter, drill holes through up to two feet of solid ice, and jig for the lake trout below. If that's not true big-fish dedication, I don't know what is! Next time you think you've got a rough October day on Rutland, think again!

The guides I fished with were both professionals, Hank Gutz from Wyoming, and 20-year-old Reinwell. You would think the older Hank would be the one using the traditional method of flatfishing, but the reverse is true. Hank runs all the latest sounders and downrigger systems, while Reinwell sticks with the older method of wire lining with the flatfish. They both have a tremendous success rate for big fish. Hank has caught 100 lb of fish in a day, all around the 6-lb mark, his largest weighing $35^{1}/_{2}$ lb. The Utah State record lake trout was taken off Linwood, at an incredible $41^{1}/_{2}$ lb, which with browns to $33^{1}/_{2}$ lb and rainbows to 27 lb make this possibly the world's best trout fishery if you want really big fish.

At the dam end of Flaming Gorge the Green River roars through the sluice at a pressure you just wouldn't believe. When I was there the generators were only letting a mere 3500 cubic feet per second through, which made a raft trip downriver for river browns a possibility. It has an average running total of 5750 cubic feet per second, boosted by snowmelt water in the spring runoff to a

Where to Fish Trout

This is one of the true giants of the trout world. Arizona trout man Dale Slocum hooked this monster lake trout on Canada's Great Bear Lake using a Mepp's lure and 12 lb line. The fish weighed in at a staggering 48 lb and illustrates what the author states about big trout needing to fulfil a predatory diet. (Photo credit to International Game Fish Association.)

staggering 7000 cubic feet per *second*! Quite how any browns below the dam survive this torrent is beyond me, but they do. Ardent fishermen can stay at a place called Flaming Gorge Lodge, run by the Colletts at Dutch John. This is a lodge, tackle store and restaurant, and offers raft trips from below the dam on the Green River. It's only thirty dollars or so for three people in a raft, and I can promise you the run down over the rapids is electrifying. There is no guide, you just learn really quickly! The scenery through the gorges is out of this world, and the markings on the brown trout quite the most superb I have ever seen. There are hordes of small rainbows in the cold depths. The Colletts have run raft trips on the river for twenty years, and the reason for being based here is not just because it is one of the most beautiful places in the state of Utah, but because you have the choice of going out on Flaming Gorge for the monster trout with a pro guide, or shooting the rapids on a raft in the Green River, stopping whenever you fancy a spot of fishing. You get dropped in with a raft just below the dam, and picked out at a prearranged collection point several miles downriver. The average river temperature ranges between 40 and 46 degrees, and boasts a sporadic mayfly hatch, depending on temperature. The bottom is messy with rocks, boulders and gravel, but it's loaded with freshwater shrimp, getting more prolific the further downstream from the dam you go. Remember that the dam wall is an amazing 550 feet high, and the Flaming Gorge Lodge set at 7000 feet above sea level.

What about the untapped potential for really big browns, and even rainbows, in the British Isles? Most of the big wild browns, or ferox as they are known, come from the big lochs on trolled spoons. Occasionally somebody picks up a big double-figure fish on a modern plug. But there must be some monsters there as well. What sport could be had by an enterprising angler who sets himself up with the big trout gear as used by the pro guides in Flaming Gorge! A colour sounder could be used to pinpoint either the coarse fish shoals which must surely form a part of a big brown's diet, or the powan shoals, which again must represent some percentage of a ferox's intake. If you don't have the baitfish, then look for a colour sounder that can show an individual fish. How do you get down to them, assuming they are anything from thirty feet down? You use a

Where to Fish Trout

British stock pond reared Rainbows can be pushed to a similar weight as that achieved in the large American open waters, but being fed on a high protein diet, they cannot maintain that weight on insect life alone. Fish like this brace of big double figure fly-caught British Rainbows are now commonplace, and are a credit to the ability of the fish farmer to rear them to this size.

downrigger system, and run deep swimming plugs like Rapalas. If they can do it in the United States, there is every possibility they can do it here. Deep jigging may also be a possibility, but I fancy trolling as better for deep-water browns. The bottoms of some of these lochs are cluttered with snags and boulders, so wire line fishing with the flatfish plugs could mean a lot of problems with snags. The bottoms of many American reservoirs are formed in smooth canyon walls. This gradually breaks down to a fine mud, which makes the flatfish so efficient at sending up puffs of mud as it digs into the bottom.

You couldn't use them on a big loch, but why can't our larger reservoirs like Rutland and Grafham allow at least a limited period of experimental fishing for the big browns and rainbows which are known to be down deep, and out of the reach of cored fly lines? A fast-sink, cored flyline can sink vertically only twenty yards if you cast out and let it drop down. Then you are confined to only a vertical retrieve, which is exactly the same as deep jigging. There would be a lateral line the lure could cover if flatfishing was allowed on the cleaner bottom of the reservoirs. Of course deep jigging is a definite possibility at these venues. Many of these super fish remain uncaught because we are not allowed to use techniques designed specifically for catching them. Certainly some British records must live and die in the depths without ever seeing an angler's fly. How about running flatfish along the bottom of somewhere like Datchet? It is a superb water giving up some beautiful wild fish; as a concrete bowl, there must be some sedimentation on the bottom, uncluttered by snags, and offering conditions surely ideal for trolling with wire lines and flatfish plugs. You may think it's food for thought, but until we attempt to change some of our policies to allow at least some sort of experimentation, it will remain just that.

There is a further lesson to be learned from the Green River browns. Other than the small hatchery rainbows, which are stocked, the browns are mostly regenerating fish. There is a strict size limit on fish that can be retained, in an attempt to maintain a stock of truly wild fish. The trout my wife Hilary and I landed were all returned, and there is no doubt at all that they can survive being caught. I think fishermen should be given the choice of returning fish, rather than assume that everything they hook must be knocked on the head. As

To slow the boat's drift down on large open reservoirs the use of a canvas drogue is advisable. Coupled to a rudder, you can govern both the pace and area you want to drift through.

stupid as rainbow trout are, they do retain limited knowledge of capture, and make a better angling challenge next time round. I have fished the White River in Arkansas, below Buffalo dam, where the water runoff was so cold there was a thick fog in the valley, with 70° temperatures up on the hills. In deep holes in this shallow gravel river lie monster wild browns. And this even when the shallow river is fished heavily by pro guides. The largest wild brown I saw weighed over 33 lb! The rainbows had an affinity for sweetcorn legered on the bottom, and the big browns of course made a diet of the rainbow. Now perhaps you can see why I think there may be monster trout in our own large waters, far bigger than anyone could have dreamed.

Where to Fish Trout

Here we have a situation where a 20-lb brown is pumped up on high-protein pellets to break a record, but the fish is stocked in just a few acres of water. As soon as it loses the protein diet it has enjoyed over the last six years, it will start to drop in weight. There simply is no way a big brown, or rainbow for that matter, can sustain such a body weight by sipping in insect larvae. How did the big mackinaws, rainbows and browns sustain their weights? They ate other small fish, especially small rainbows! Imagine a batch of browns growing on in somewhere like Rutland or Grafham. They get past the insect-eating stage, and reach 3 lb, when they need some protein like fry to keep up their weight gains. They do this and get much bigger, but have to expend more energy in catching sticklebacks than these baitfish give them in protein. Just when their weights would naturally level off, along comes the stocking truck and dumps in a few thousand fingerlings, all nice sized mouthfuls for a big brown. You can see why I now think there may be some incredible creatures swimming about in the deep waters. The Americans have the technology. We have the potential in the shape of undiscovered depths. Think lures. Think deep. And think *big* trout!

Facing page: In boat-fishing conditions it is unwise to stand, especially in a narrow beam boat like this. If you do need to stand to cast, make sure your partner remains seated. Bewl Bridge Reservoir is the venue and this angler fishes a sunk line for Rainbows.

Go Fishing for Trout

Even on relatively small waters that are stocked regularly with trout, you can reach fish better by using a boat. It allows you to present your fly to a trout from a different angle than a bank fisherman. These two anglers are fishing the main water of Bayham Abbey Lake in Sussex.

Fly Fishing

Having explained the various other methods available to the trout enthusiast, I have to cover ground steeped in tradition. Fly fishing, as far as I am concerned, is a method devised to protect the trout. They could be taken on other methods a lot more easily, but the art of fly fishing is a technique which presents an insect imitation on, or under, the surface film, and that imitation is uncastable by normal fishing methods. There is a method called dapping, but that still does not involve casting, only allowing the wind to billow out the fly and fly line.

For fly fishing you can use the weight of the fly line to carry the leader and fly out to the fish, and I can say that the casting in itself, once learned, is very enjoyable. It's akin to riding a bicycle, something you never forget. At first it seems as though you will never get it right, with coils of line lashing your ears, and hooks stuck in clothing. All you have to remember is that even top fly casters had to learn somewhere, some time, and the sooner you start the better. One basic I would advise learning well, is timing. If somebody teaches you, you will learn it, but if learning on your own or from a casting instruction manual, just make sure you watch the backcast unroll, and try to slow everything down the further out the line is.

Tackle

An important advance is being made in the development of fly lines, and their behaviour under a wide variety of fishing conditions. The company responsible for this new fly line technology is Airflo. They can supply you with a technical information service second to none concerning their range of lines. To suit the different fishing conditions, fly lines come in varying weights and tapers. This is called the AFTM rating. The two most common types of fly line tapers are called the double taper, and the weight forward. With a double taper the centre section of the line remains at a constant diameter. At either end the diameter tapers down, which apart from assisting the fly leader to unroll at the completion of the cast, means you can turn the line round and use the other end if the first starts showing signs of wear. For beginners a double taper is usually advised, but I am afraid that I would disagree. A weight forward line has most of the width and line weight towards one end of the fly line, tapering down as it is wound around the reel drum. Weight forwards, once mastered, are easier to cast with, as having that extra weight away from the rod tip, you need fewer false casts to achieve your required distance.

A fly will act as a drag force throughout the false casting and actually have some effect on the leader's unrolling ability should the fly be heavily dressed and weighted. An overweight nymph on the other hand will be too heavy to unroll the leader properly, and a lighter AFTM-rated fly line may not be able to impart enough impetus to carry the weighted nymph out to the extent of the leader. The AFTM ratings are carried in numbers from 1 to 12, and matched accordingly by fly rods manufactured by the tackle industry. A number 1 line is used, if at all, for very light fishing on brooks or streams where hardly any casting distance is required. A number 12 would be a lot heavier, and therefore be used with a correspondingly powerful rod for long casting, saltwater fishing, and some specialised freshwater lakes will require the number 11 and 12. Perhaps the norm for trout fishing in the past fifty years would have dropped to between 5 and 6. But now, with the larger waters and greater distances required, I would suggest a 7 or 8 as the normal weight. I believe the heavier lines of 7 and 8 are easier for beginners to learn with as they become accustomed to making the weight of the flyline stress up the rod for the cast. Airflo fly lines have virtually no stretch compared with the PVC models, and this is important if you want to cast well.

As well as having an AFTM weight number as a regulation, fly lines can also be made to fish different layers of the water. This is important if you are to locate the trout's feeding depth. For a variety of reasons the fish may be feeding exclusively in one particular strip of water. They may be grubbing on the bottom after snails, or cruising across weedbeds picking off shrimps. They can be rising towards the surface taking hatching nymphs, or they can actually take a floating insect off the surface film. This latter feeding pattern is termed a 'rise'. The majority of these feeding patterns will apply to 'wild' fish, i.e. those hatched from an egg by a naturalised fish, or a stocked fish of small size that has been introduced to grow on under its own steam.

I am extremely doubtful whether many put-and-take trout fisheries have a resident stock of naturalised trout that develop into all the feeding categories. Many are fish stocked at large sizes after being fed on in a stock pond on trout protein pellets. They are often caught just a few hours after being stocked, and as you can imagine, represent little in the way of angling skill. To illustrate this, you can stand at most of the day ticket waters with a line of anglers all casting at the area they think has received the stock fish. An angler takes a fish on a black lure, then the person next to him has one on white, the next man on a yellow lure. This tells you absolutely nothing about the colour preference of the fish, except that they have none! The same group of anglers can hit fish, yards apart, on lead-headed jigs, tiny nymphs, big lures, at depths from one foot to the lake bed. It tells you nothing about feeding depths, simply because there aren't any. Those fish have been used to a diet of pellets, several times a day, 365 days a year. With big fish, this may last for four years. With several thousand fish in a stock pond, they get a split second to take the pellet, otherwise it will be gone forever; something like survival of the quickest! Take that same trout, which if it is over 8 lb may have been fed up to 4380 times or more, and you can see that the very first thing

Spooning a trout to find out what it has been feeding on is only of use when the fish has become established in a water over several weeks, or is a true wild fish. Although you may not have an exact imitation of the natural insect, you can at least attempt to duplicate colour and size.

Above: A simple plastic marrow spoon does the job of revealing stomach contents, but there's little point when you fish a water that has daily stocking – all you will find in the trout are trout pellets that it was fed on a few hours earlier!

Right: These snails were spooned from a Hampshire trout that had been introduced as a stockfish a season earlier. During the winter when insect life was at its lowest ebb, it had fed on the bottom, gorging itself on these snails. If you hit a fish that has got snails in it, you can be sure the trout are feeding deep, and that's the place to put your fly or bait.

that passes in front of its nose is likely to be grabbed! Hardly an indication of angling skill.

However, once a few fish are pricked, broken off or generally frightened off, they begin to realise that they are not going to be spoon fed any more, and have to resort to other food. This food may be limited to different depths, even right down to the bottom, and this is when you need to make the correct choice as to the weight of line you wish to use. Once the trout drops into a feeding area, he is unlikely to move far out of it, until that food source dries up.

The Americans who fish crank baits for black bass call this the 'kill zone'. A professional tournament bass fisherman will fish his crank bait through that defined 'kill zone' many more times than you or I. This gives him the ability to pick up that bonus fish and optimise his fishing time to achieve the best results. I would advise you to think along those same lines. Where are the trout feeding? Select a line that will fish your fly in that area, or 'kill zone'.

As I have mentioned, Airflo make a vast range of top quality lines, most of a revolutionary advanced design that will change fly fishing. The competition must be concerned at this advance, because for once British products could well dominate the world market in their field. Airflo ranges through all the different line weights, starting at the surface fishing end. Their Plus Floating line comes in a double taper 5–9, in 30-yard length and peach colour, or a weight forward 5–9. The Super Plus Floating line comes in double tapers 3–12, 30 yards, tan colour or weight forward 3–12, 30 yards tan or fluorescent. Their Super Plus Intermediate is really a neutral density line available in double tapers 4–10, 30 yards long, coloured green, or in weight forward 4–12, 30 yards, in green. To get sufficiently below the surface film you need the Airflo Super Plus slow sink, which is available as a weight forward 4–9, 30 yards long, and watery blue/green in colour. Next is the Super Plus lure/streamer, available in a weight forward 6–9, 35 yards long and watery blue/green in colour. To get well down in the surface layers you are going to need a line like the Super Plus fast sink which comes in three line shapes. The double taper offers 5–11 in 30 yards, dark brown colour. The weight forward offers 5–11 in 30 yards and dark brown. Then there is a steep taper for 6–11 in 35 feet and dark brown colour. For most of the trout fishing in rivers, lakes and small fisheries you need only a small selection of these lines.

Obviously you are not going to need every single model of line, but a suggestion for starting fly fishing would be to get yourself three lines. Assuming you have already chosen a rod that throws a line weight of 6–8, you would be well advised to stick to line weights of 7. Get yourself a floating line for dry fly and surface film nymph presentation. Then a slow sink line for fishing just in the first two feet of water, and a fast sink line for getting the fly, nymph or lure down near the bottom where that 'kill zone' might be. Should you boat fish from some of the larger open bodies of water like our big freshwater reservoirs, you will need further lines to reach the 'kill zone', sometimes many feet beneath the hull of the boat. Airflo can cope with this problem as well, offering their Super Plus super fast sinker in a weight forward 8–13, 30 yards long and charcoal grey in colour. There is also a steep taper of 8–13 in 35-foot lengths and charcoal grey colour. You will no doubt have realised that such line weights are going to need a new rod to cast them with, as big reservoirs are subject to wind, and casting can be difficult. Their final fast sink range is called the Super Plus Depth Charge, and are really for specialised fishing, for something like big browns in very deep water. These lines come in grain weights and steep tapers, all in 35-foot lengths, and weights of 550, 750 and 900 grains. Colours are dark brown, charcoal grey or black.

Most of the lines mentioned are full-length fly lines, but for this last specialised form of fishing you will use a much shorter length of fly line that is attached to a backing line. This short fly line is called a shooting head, and is designed for long distance casting with a heavy weight floating or sinking fly line. The backing can be flat nylon, dacron or braided nylon. Flat line in monofilament is quite good, dacron can lead to some terrible tangles unless you take care to lay it out before each cast. Which leaves braided line as my idea of the best backing material.

The new technology offered by Airflo lines has many breakthroughs that benefit the ordinary angler. Much of it is heavy scientific jargon, but it's important to remember what I feel is the best advantage to using an Airflo. Most fly lines are PVC and have a considerable amount of stretch in them. Many anglers feel this margin of stretch in the line is ideal for not breaking a fish off, and that a non-stretch line makes the leader tippet snap. To a certain extent this may be true, but the shock-absorbing quality of stretchy fly lines will also prevent you from feeling many delicate takes, particularly if you are fishing a slow retrieve. You can actually have a trout take the fly in and spit it out so gently you feel nothing. With the non-stretch Airflo this is reduced to such an extent that you feel everything going on at the fly end, and can lift straight into a fish, even on a long line. As for the problem of break-offs, the fishing rod, apart from being a casting tool, acts as a buffer and will cushion most of the critical stages of any fish fight. The only real danger comes

Keep checking your line guides which may chip if dropped, or wear through like this metal ring which was so badly grooved by line friction it eventually cut a flyline in half! Replace it if in any doubt.

Fly Fishing

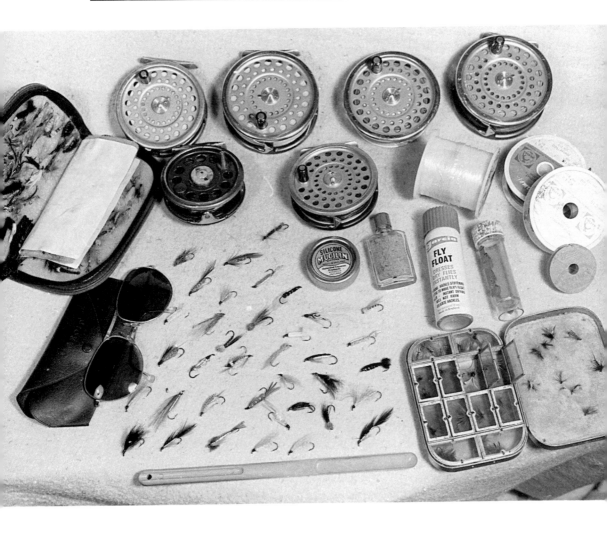

The trout angler who fishes the fly rod needs a basic armoury of tackle. Besides a rod and landing net (and a priest if the fish is killed), everything else that is needed is in this picture.

when you are just about to finish a retrieve and hit a fish on a short line. An experienced angler reacts more quickly than a novice, and there is no real way if you are a beginner to 'sense' that you shouldn't strike too hard with a non-stretch line at close range. When you strike a fish on a long line much of the energy is stored within the rod, and within the line itself. A stretchy PVC line illustrates this, so a line that cannot absorb so much stretch transmits your strike to the hook, hopefully inserting it into the fish.

Some consideration must be given to the leader or tippet. This is a tapered length of nylon that is attached to the end of the fly line, usually about nine feet in length, the other end being attached to the hook. You can purchase ready-made tapered leaders, or you can taper them down yourself using stages of different diameter nylon monofilament. To couple their lines to leaders, Airflo produces its own special braided leader material. They are more supple than monofilament, and turn over at the end of the cast superbly, and absorb shock. Another advantage of the Airflo leader system is knotless quick-release fly line connection, where previously you would have to permanently needle knot a butt length of heavy mono. There are also fewer wind knots, better casting directly into the wind and virtually no memory from reel storage. They are available in a wide range of lengths and knotless leaders. They make a floating leader that rests high on the surface film to register the slightest take. This matches their floating fly line range. They offer an intermediate leader that sinks very slowly. You can treat them with braid float to make them float, or braid sink, to get them under the surface film. Their fast-sinking leader range takes the fly down extremely fast, and dispenses with the need for sink tip fly lines, offering more tactical advantages to fly presentation. Many fast sink leaders can contain metal wire or lead core, but Airflo braided leaders contain no lead. Instead they have a polymer in them containing a material twice as heavy as lead. These fast sink leaders can be used on floating, intermediate and fast sink fly lines, and all feature the no-knot quick attachment system. The range on offer is as follows. Floating comes in a gradual taper. Intermediate in gradual, steep and salmon steelhead taper, finally the fast-sinking leaders come in gradual taper, steep taper and salmon/steelhead taper.

Fly Fishing

Flies

When fly fishing it is advisable to have a very basic understanding of insect life. While many of the day ticket put-and-take trout hardly get time to take any insects, there may come a time when you are fishing a reservoir, river or loch where the trout have grown on naturally, or fishing a put-and-take fishery where for a number of reasons a few occupants have evaded capture and have begun to take insects as part of their diet. Into this category fall fish that are returned alive despite the rule in most put-and-take fisheries that all fish caught must be killed. Not every angler kills every single trout, and the more successful anglers will often slip the odd fish back. There are also a few catch-and-release trout fisheries where the fish have learned to take natural insect life. Of course I would not consider a

The basic fly shape that catches stock-reared trout: throat hackle, contrasting body colours and a tail. Even this nymph pattern designed by the author lends itself to fly fishing. If it catches trout, then use it!

double-figure rainbow as a naturalised trout feeding exclusively on insects. A big fish doesn't either grow big, or retain or maintain any sort of body weight in that category without undertaking a more substantial diet. A trout, either brown or rainbow, will be likely to feed on insects from the weight of $1/2$ lb up to 4 lb. Anything above that weight will need to be sustained by larger prey, and they undoubtedly resort to either feeding on snails, or turn completely predatory and eat other small fish. As I mentioned earlier, in America the huge rainbows, lakes and browns have been found with other rainbow trout jammed down their gullets. In fact my opinion is that the brown will turn predator a lot quicker than the rainbow, although the rainbow will still be the more gullible feeder, even on insects.

While most insects are unsavoury to us, a few are worth acquainting yourself with as the end product of such an ac-quaintanceship can often be a trout on the bank. I have no interest in the structural characteristics of the 30-odd orders of insects. Some anglers make a life career out of studying their life systems, and even develop their artificial fly tying to a level only understood by themselves. Personally I think they are over-complicating matters as you only need one fly, and that's the one the trout takes. Pike fishing today is done very much with artificial lures, and lure fishermen would be among the first to admit that it is the collection of lures, rather than their productivity that keeps them interested. I myself have a collection of marlin lures that I consider as my 'babies'. There are different designs, colours, weights, actions, designed for cloudy days, bright, windy, flat conditions etc. Yet now, after many years of fishing artificial lures for marlin, I could probably pick out just four patterns, and four colours, then go anywhere that holds marlin, and catch one. But I too, still like playing with the others!

The most important of the insect orders to the trout angler is the Ephemeroptera, of which there are sixty or seventy species. This adult insect has a transparent wing membrane with two pairs, those at the rear being smaller than those at the front. When perched on a branch or leaf the wings are held vertically, which gives rise to their name 'upwinged flies'. The classic example of this is the mayfly. These can be particularly prolific in May and June. Their life cycle is worth noting. The adult flies are seen in aerial swarms at rivers or

Fly Fishing

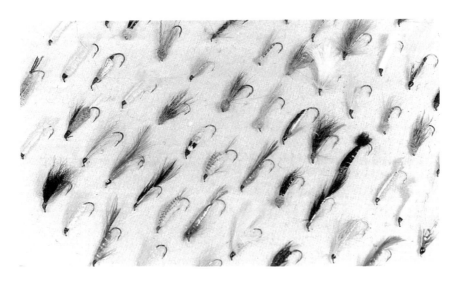

Above: A good selection of flies seems to be a basic requirement of all fly fishermen but the author feels that six patterns will suffice on small streams and stillwaters, with another six patterns for reservoir work. All you then need change is the hook size and colours of those patterns. Flies probably catch more fly fishermen than they do trout!

Right: Tying your own pattern of fly makes an interesting winter pastime, allowing you to create variations on traditional patterns like these reverse hackled Mayflies for dry fly fishing. Or let your imagination run riot and tie up what you feel might be successful.

lakeside, where after mating the females lay their eggs in batches. At this stage they are called spinners. The eggs stick firmly to the bottom and later hatch out as nymphs. After mating the adults die and fall on the surface where they are called spent flies. Obviously when these dead insects are floating about on the surface the trout soon cash in on the easy feed. The various species of nymphs obviously vary, but they all have three hair-like tails which distinguish them from the other orders. As well as taking the dead adults off the surface, the trout soon become aware of the bottom-to-surface rise of nymphs that begin the mating life cycle again up to two years from egg laying. When the nymphs reach the surface the outer skin splits and the winged insect struggles free. Although capable of flight at this stage, it still has another skin to shed, and is called a dun. Usually this second skin shed takes place on a leaf, tree or bush, and you can actually watch it happen at the peak of the hatch. The dun is fairly colourless, but when it emerges again as an adult or spinner the pigments in the body are richer, and those upright wings have a sheen and delicacy to marvel at. For the dry fly fisherman fishing his imitation on top of the surface film, and the nymph angler fishing his imitation just beneath the surface film, this is the most important order of flies.

Another popular order is the Trichoptera. The larvae of these insects construct tubular cases of threads of silk around their bodies to which they stick sand grains, shells, twig debris and bits of leaf. On the lake or river bed they can only be seen by an enthusiastic fisherman, and even as they crawl along the bottom, they form part of the trout's diet. When fully grown the larvae pupate and emerge on reed and weed stems as winged adult insects called sedges. Important variations of fly dressings, particularly colour toning, will often mean the difference between catching trout and enjoying a blank session.

The third order is the Plecoptera. These nymphs have only two tails, and some of the larger species devour caddis larvae and other nymphs. The adults have crossed-over wings across the back of the body when at rest, which are hard and shiny, unlike the gossamer frailness of the mayflies.

Although there are many other orders of insect life, these three will give enough variation with regard to tying or buying artificial

Facing page: Top writer Graeme Pullen enjoys fishing the fly for trout but accepts there are many other methods the fisherman can enjoy.

Above: The mighty Green River, below the Flaming Gorge Dam in the State of Utah adopts a release limitation policy on all its trout. The author (left) gently returns a Green River Wild Brown to its home of splendour. Although we cannot boast trout fishing in such magnificent scenery in the UK, the policy of killing all trout must surely change, giving the angler the option on whether he wants to return the fish or not. Hilary Pullen (right) with a superbly marked wild Brown trout taken on a small Mepps spinner in a pool below one of the rapids. This trout was released.

Left: In America you can fish for both Browns and Rainbows with a variety of weird baits. Here is a selection used by the author on the White River and Red River in the State of Arkansas. They include Wireworm grubs, marshmallows and coloured salmon eggs!

Above: A trout pond on the Portuguese island of Madeira. The Rainbows all swim in one direction so the angler can often present his fly to a stocked Rainbow in a fishery after waiting for it to appear on its circular route again. Don't chase after the fish when casting – wait until it comes round again.

Right: Stock ponds in the State of Utah where the rare Albino Rainbow is grown. Such a species may prove difficult in British waters where the colour makes them susceptible to the Heron.

The Brook trout enjoys very cold water and was stocked as a popular fish in the late 1970s. Their failure to adapt to our warm, shallow water fisheries in summer caused them to lie at the bottom of lakes where temperatures were coolest. They would be better stocked in cold rivers in the north of England and are fine fighters when in prime condition. They have a distinctive white flash to the leading edge of all ventral, pectoral and anal fins.

Left: This is Britain's largest Brown trout, an artificially reared fish from Dever Springs in Hampshire. It was stocked at over 22 lbs but will lose weight rapidly as there is insufficient baitfish to make it maintain or increase weight.

Right: An exclusive picture for this book. Centre back is a world-record, fly-caught wild Rainbow of over 27 lbs. Bottom left is a massive previous world record Brown trout, again a wild fish, of 34 lbs, and bottom right Graeme's wife Hilary holds a 35 lb Lake or Mackinaw trout. These all came from Utah's Flaming Gorge Reservoir.

Look at the clear, crisp markings on this wild brownie taken from a stream. Small fish like these may be many years old and rarely top 1 lb in weight, especially if they live in acid streams with little food. They are fine sport on light tackle and take baits as well as fly.

The Rainbow, as held by the author, from Rockbourne Trout Fishery in Hampshire, is the prime species of trout sought by flyfishing. They grow fast, fight well, and will take virtually any bait, lure or fly.

Although predatory, the Brown trout will still fall for a small fly. Nobody really knows why this should be so but I think they would be caught more easily from large reservoirs if methods and restrictions were relaxed – if only for an experimental period.

Above: You will catch more fish in a stream or river when approaching from downstream, so you come up behind the fish. This angler is casting upstream to a rising fish and is using the rushbed in front of him for additional cover.

Right: In contrast, casting the fly downstream allows the current to straighten the leader and therefore eliminates many presentation problems. I suggest it is far more effective than fishing upstream if a long cast is used to keep distance between angler and fish.

Below: Care should be exercised when wading and approaching fish with dry fly. A fish is rising under this bough and the fisherman dare not get closer for fear of spooking it.

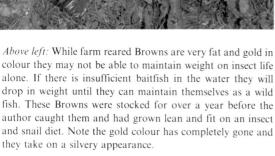

Above left: While farm reared Browns are very fat and gold in colour they may not be able to maintain weight on insect life alone. If there is insufficient baitfish in the water they will drop in weight until they can maintain themselves as a wild fish. These Browns were stocked for over a year before the author caught them and had grown lean and fit on an insect and snail diet. Note the gold colour has completely gone and they take on a silvery appearance.

Above right: Of all the trout species, the Rainbow is the most popular because of its rapid growth rate in artificial rearing conditions. Good fish farms can produce superb Rainbows like this specimen from Willinghurst Fishery at Bramley in Surrey.

Right: (Above) The Mayfly is the most famous of the trout fisherman's flies and occurs for just three weeks each year. In that time the trout lose all caution and the fisherman never has a better chance. (Below) A rare picture of a hatching Damsel fly together with its old shuck.

Facing page: A selection of tackle from years ago. Modern tackle technology has ensured that the art of presenting a fly to a trout is far easier than a hundred years ago. However the principle is still unchanged and the angler will need the same stealthy approach to induce that take.

Above: Graeme Pullen shows off a superb wild Irish Brown Trout of $3^1/_2$ lbs before returning it alive for another angler to catch. The fish took freelined lobworm.

Facing page: The Brown trout is our natural species but has been superseded by the fast growing Rainbow. Where both species are stocked together, the free biting Rainbow will range far and wide in the water, while the Brown will start to become territorial and feed on baitfish faster than the Rainbow.

Facing page: The author lifts off into a Rainbow at Langford Fisheries using the dry fly. The fish need to be spotted, or a rise seen, then a cast made presenting the dry fly as near the trout's position as possible. (Inset) When a trout takes on a dry fly, always wait a couple of seconds for them to turn down with that fly, otherwise you'll miss them every time. Experience with timing is the only thing to make your technique productive.

Above: The method of upstream nymph fishing needs every bit as much care in approach and presentation as when dry fly fishing. Keep as far from the fish's position as possible and place the nymph slightly to one side of him so the leader doesn't spook him.

equivalents, more than you are likely to use properly in a single season. If these insects are hatching out, and both time of year and temperature dictate when this will happen, identification is made easy. You can pick up one of the insects and even if you cannot put a positive classification to it, you should be able to establish it within one of the three orders. Then you simply take the nearest matching fly from your box, and fish with it. Sometimes the trout will have what is known as a preoccupation, and then you will catch only by using an exact match to the real thing. When no flies are seen to be hatching, there will be no trout 'rise' so isolation of individual fish becomes more time consuming. It's best then to assume the trout are looking either for stone flies, or carnivorous nymphs, or searching mid-water for nymphs working their way towards the surface. Then you should fish under the surface with any choice of nymph that takes your fancy. Assuming you get lucky and hit a fish, the next stage after killing it (should this be what you want) is to spoon it. This means pushing a plastic or metal marrow scoop down its throat as far as possible, twisting it, then slowly sliding it out. You should have a few insects in the scoop, which if you cannot identify them positively, will at least give you something to match up to from your nymph selection.

With the thousands of different natural insects about, you can appreciate how many different flies there are in an angler's wallet! For a dry fly selection to start with, a few of the older traditional patterns are still very good. After all, the change in fashion with tackle suppliers is a lot faster than the ecological change in the insect life chain! Try a few of these as stand-bys in your wallet: Black Gnat, Pheasant Tail, March Brown, Silver Sedge, Iron Blue Dun and Ginger Quill. Traditional wet flies like March Brown, Gold-Ribbed Hare's Ear, Wickham's Fancy and Black Spider will produce to a sunk line on both river and lake. Others like Jersey Herd, Butcher and Alexandra are also fish takers. Remember these are patterns to try for fully naturalised, partially naturalised, or forced naturalised (stocked water) trout, both browns and rainbows.

Traditional wet flies can be used in teams. Fished two or three at a time it allows you to put a different fly on each dropper and cut down on the time needed to find out the best pattern. In some of the big

Facing page: The author throws a line for an early season Welsh trout up in the Brecon Beacons. A dusting of snow still lies on the hills. On small reservoirs the baitfish population may not be large enough to maintain growth rates on record fish but in really big waters there is every chance of a double figure wild fish, if various methods, other than flyfishing, are allowed.

open still waters you can still use this method, but on the small stocked waters it is banned entirely. This is because if an angler breaks off a fish, it will be towing around two other flies along its flanks. The stocked fish are so gullible they simply rush over and grab the other flies and you then have two fish hooked and struggling against each other until they tucker out and die. On these waters the stocking density is incredibly high, and another fish could even be hooked at the same time as the first!

Dry Fly Fishing

In dry fly fishing, you must remember a cardinal rule. Never strike too early. I well remember my first true dry fly trout as a youngster at Damerham trout lakes near Fordingbridge in Hampshire. This venue is noted for its incredible mayfly hatch due to the pure water springs that feed it, and I had been struggling all day. My problem was that I had no mayfly nymphs with which to tempt the trout during the day, so by the time the lunchtime rise on duns began I was almost tearing my hair out. I decided pride would have to take a back seat, and walked back to the fishing lodge to ask owner Colin Harms if he would sell me a dry mayfly. This he did, not just a regular shop-bought variety, but a special mayfly tied by a local fly tyer, specially for this season at Damerham. It would simply slaughter them he told me. I greased the leader, changed to a floating line (I was on a sinker, which was the cause of my problem!) tied on the mayfly, sprayed it with flotant and cast at everything that made a rise. Obviously if I threw at enough rises I would be near a trout, but I had no polaroid glasses, and thus couldn't see what was going on beneath the surface. By the evening rise I must have missed a dozen rises, and my strikes were getting faster and faster in my frantic effort to sink a hook in.

It was late evening and I was the last angler left on the top lake, at that time newly dug. The spinners were spent and the surface was littered with bodies of mayflies. The occasional rise was still underway, but with less of a frenzy as the trout had gorged themselves. In the failing light I made one last cast, let the fly settle, and saw a rise underneath it. I shut my eyes, paused a second and struck. That fish weighed 1 lb 14 ozs, and gave me the best lesson in dry fly striking. Never, ever strike too early. Let the fish close its mouth and turn down before setting the hook. It is easier said than done, and even this past season, with rather more trout in the net since those early days, I was boat fishing Newbury Trout Lakes in Berkshire, with my partner Adrian Hutchins. We had picked up a few fish between the islands when a giant bumble bee whipped onto the surface and sent out concentric rings as it tried vainly to take off. We both watched it for a second, then right in front of our noses a rainbow sucked in the bee! We changed to dry fly, and I missed six fish in my excitement!

If you fish the dry fly a lot you'll get very good at it, even equalling or surpassing the subsurface nymph fisherman. But it's not easy. It really does take a little skill. Not that it's superior or ethically better to take a trout on a dry fly. It is merely another method for the trout enthusiast to use, but it does have a satisfying quality when you lift off a floating line and connect with a fish.

Lake fishing is comparatively easy with a dry fly. You simply throw it out and wait. If it's windy you throw directly into the wind, or downwind. If you throw across wind you can get line drag, which means the fly will skate over the surface unnaturally. Only once have I seen a dragged dry fly take fish, and that was at Leominstead fishery in the New Forest. There used to be an artificially moored island at one end and an American tourist was dragging a huge Stateside dry bug over the surface like a wake fly. It was glassy calm and we all giggled at his method. He soon took the smile off our faces when we saw him go back for his third ticket!

I recently walked up to Bob Church, probably Britain's best-known trout man, fishing on Willow Lake at Dever Springs. Fishing had been slow, and Bob was throwing out a dry mayfly and stripping it in under the surface. It was no real surprise to see him hit a 3-lb rainbow, and it just goes to show that no theory is always 100 per cent correct.

River or stream fishing with the dry fly is a little more demanding.

You have a moving body of water to contend with, and perhaps wind as well. You will be casting to a stationary fish in the current that you have spotted visually, or have marked down by its rise. You may have faster currents in front of you, and slower currents where the fish is. You can always mend the cast by flicking a loop of line back upstream of the fast water once you have made a cast, but the best way to avoid this, is to get as directly below the fish as you can. That will not only put your line across less varied current paces, but it will further conceal you from the fish. Also when you strike, your direction of pull will be in opposition to the fish, and should give a better hookhold. Dry fly fishing is an interesting technique but don't let yourself get too bogged down in entomology. Keep to the three orders of flies mentioned, and use them mostly in the months of May through to September when rises are best.

Nymphing

A far more productive method on both lakes and rivers is nymphing. Let us deal with rivers and streams first. The best way, without a shadow of a doubt, on larger rivers is downstream wet fly fishing. Don't cast directly across the current to the other bank, but make your cast slightly downstream. The current immediately takes control of the line and will belly it round in an arc. Let it do this, and retrieve only when the flies are stationary in the current directly below you. If you have to wade in, do so carefully, avoiding any undue splashing that may disturb the fish. If the flies race round too quickly you may have to flick a loop of line back upstream to 'mend' the cast and slow the fly travel down a bit.

If you fish rocky mountain streams, the fish will probably be in tiny holding pools where the current eddies, making food location a bit easier. To stop your flies being whisked away too soon, pinch a shot just up from the fly and keeping the rod high, make the fly stay in the tiny area, maybe behind a rock, for as long as possible. The Americans call this 'pocket fishing', and it can be used upstream or

Late afternoon is an ideal time to look for trout nymphing in the surface film. These anglers have taken advantage of a good ripple to work a floating line in towards a bay.

down. Most rivers and small streams have a compulsory approach rule of fishing nymphs upstream only. That means you start at the lower section of the river beat and work your way upstream, casting at fish or likely-looking lies as you go. This is purely ethical, because years ago it was thought you would catch too many fish by fishing the fly downstream. The latter method is highly productive, but I have to say that working upstream on a small stream is an advantage in itself. I hate being told how I should fish, but take a walk down a small stream and see how many trout bolt as they see you. By walking from downstream upriver you will be coming up behind the fish, and therefore be in a position to present your nymph without his ever having any knowledge that you are there. Of course you will have to retrieve line to stay in contact as the fly travels down with the current, otherwise you can't feel when a trout takes.

Visual striking is possible when you can actually see the response of the trout, but coloured water makes it impossible to see. Then you must rely on watching the leader where it enters the water, or the end of the fly line. Any stops could well be a fish so strike at anything halting the downstream progress of the line.

Frequent casting is required when you fish upstream nymphs, and watch for any bulges or humps beneath where you think the leader is, as this is often caused by a fish following.

Two other tips are worth noting with this method. With wet fly downstream you can actually make the trout take by twitching the fly back upstream in jerks or short strips. The true art of the upstream nymph fisherman is the 'induced take'. This means that when a trout lying in the current refuses your offerings that drift past its vision, you must impart some movement to the nymph to indicate life. This is done by speeding up the retrieve as it nears the fish, and in effect making the nymph rise towards the surface.

The second method is to use a larger nymph than you know the trout are likely to see. An oversize mayfly, heavily leaded is ideal. Cast well upstream of the trout, then strip the fly downstream near the surface very fast. The trout will whip round and chase after it. If it follows for more than a couple of seconds, stop the fly dead, and the trout will often engulf it straight away. I can't tell you how many times this has given me a fish, especially the gullible, greedy rainbows. This confirms what I have said about all species of trout having a predatory instinct.

Upstream nymph fishing takes a bit out of you physically, due to the number of accurate casts you have to make. Yet it's a good way to take trout, and is worth learning well, as the strike and presentation techniques, coupled with accurate casting, will help you when you get down to visual stalking in the small lakes.

When nymph fishing on lakes, you can generally allow a lot longer to take your quota of fish on a big reservoir than you would on one of the put-and-take fisheries. For the big open waters you need to ask at the fishery lodge what hatches are taking place, what depth the trout are taking at, and which area of the reservoir they are likely to be in. There is no hard and fast rule to taking these fish, as a reservoir is a big body of water, and the fish will be wild or semi-wild. This is why it is so difficult for someone who has started trout fishing on the easy small fisheries to make the change successfully to big waters. The reservoir specialist of course soon grasps the requirements of small waters, which are so much easier due to intensive stocking.

As well as working the dam wall areas of big reservoirs, you should also take note of prevailing wind directions. It is a good idea to fish directly into the wind, as all the surface-borne food particles will have been drifted into that bank.

In the autumn you'll be wanting to try the shallow margins where coarse fish fry will be getting harassed by feeding trout. Big browns especially often leave care blowing in the wind at this time, and lose some of their caution as they chase fry in close to the dam or bank edge.

Feeding Habits

There are two incidents which illustrate how predatory the trout is. I once fished in the inflow pipe of a small trout water. A 3-lb rainbow was sitting just inside the pipe. He came out occasionally and I got enough good drops in front of his nose to realise he was treating me with derision. He was quite a famous fish, for everyone had taken a crack at him, not for his size, but because he was deemed uncatchable. Behind and below him on the gravel bottom were some sticklebacks. Every time I let the fly sink to the bottom while I waited for him to come out on his rounds, the stickles would cluster round it, though goodness knows the nymph was nearly as big as they were! I was jiggling the nymph up and down, when I decided there might be a chance of impaling one on the hook. No sooner was this done than the rainbow came out of the pipe like a heat-seeking missile, snapped up the hapless stickleback and departed back up the pipe! It was a second before I struck and the goings-on up that pipe were amazing. I was cheered on by the other anglers as my rod tip bent round in a hoop, the top of which disappeared back up the pipe.

Eventually I got the fish out, and after netting it, gently returned it. That fish had refused everything shown him, and even though he was facing up the flow of the pipe and couldn't possibly see the struggling stickle, its predatory instincts told it that there was a fish below it, and it popped out to nail it!

Another occasion I was fishing a famous big fish water which had two lakes. One held minnows as baitfish, the other sticklebacks. The average size of the stocked fish was in excess of 3 lb, and a percentage of these were browns. Some of the browns actually overwintered after being pricked and lost, but lost a lot of weight in the search for a food source other than pellets. They obviously took the odd insect, but the energy expended in catching them meant they could barely gain weight. They then found snails on the bottom and hordes of minnows around the margins. You could see these semi-wild browns cruising nonchalantly up and down in three feet of water, with the harrowed minnow shoals working as tight to the bank as they could. They were 'uncatchable' by all accounts—but I thought otherwise. I jiggled a fly on the bottom, the minnows clustered round, and I hooked one. I simply swung it out into the water where the browns were, and after a couple of flashes they were gone! The browns had dropped in weight from 3–4 lb to $1^1/2$–$1^3/4$ lb, but were in superb condition—long, lean fish with fantastic markings. Most of them I returned alive.

A feeding trout will take almost anything. About fifteen years or more ago I was having trouble convincing an angler that fly fishing was designed purely to protect the trout, which were too easy to catch. We were lying on the banks at the first lake at Damerham with another group of anglers, eating lunch and basking in the May sunshine. It was midday and everything had slowed down, including the trout which cruised up and down.

'They will take everything but the fly,' I told them, 'and I'll show you.' I walked over to Colin Harms and asked him if for the purpose of proving a point I could catch a trout and return it. He agreed, and I sat down next to the angler, and took out my last piece of currant cake. 'See this,' I said. 'The trout will even eat the currants out of this cake.' I ate some of the cake, broke off some currants and threw them at a cruising trout. Nothing happened. I did it twice more, and the next time there was mayhem as three trout followed the currants down to the bottom, gobbling them up. 'Satisfied?' I said. 'Ah well, that doesn't mean you can catch them' he said. That struck me as the sort of statement on which to place a not inconsiderable sum of money, but I refrained. Hooking two currants on I swung them out, crouched behind the rushes and waited. It took about two seconds before a mouth appeared, gulped down the currants and went looking for more. I struck and netted a two-pounder, which I returned. I put another couple of currants on, threw in some loose offerings and repeated the procedure. After the fifth trout, the owner decided I had proved my point, my critic admitted defeat, and all the other anglers were walking casually back to their cars for more packed lunches!

The late Richard Walker once wrote to me when I said I had found twigs and leaves inside trout from Avington Lakes. He explained that trout will take anything. He went on to say how he had flicked a cigarette end into a lake and seen it disappear as a trout swallowed it. So intrigued was he that he actually tied up a fly looking like a cigarette end. He even gave it his own Latin name, 'fagendus vulgaris' I think he called it. And he caught trout with it too! This shows how versatile the trout's diet is.

Go Fishing for Trout

Fishing Small Waters

Small water fishing is easy—once you know how. Small water trout have been fed for months or even years depending on how large the fishery owner wishes them to grow. The more these fish are hand fed in a stew pond, the more they come to associate humans with food. If you walk along the edge of a trout stew pond the fish will follow you up and down like a dog waiting for his meal. They associate human movement with feeding time, in complete contrast to a true wild fish, which associates human forms and movement with fear! In fact, at some venues, when you walk down to the bank at starting time the trout actually swim over to you expecting to be fed!

If you were walking beside a stew pond with the thousand or so trout in tow behind you, would you want to drop a fly to them? And if you would, how many trout would you want to catch? I'm sure that after the first two or three you would have had enough and walk away, and of course ascribe nothing in the way of angling skill to their capture. Why then, is it better to catch that same trout just hours later after it has been released into a larger lake? It's just as gullible, yet some people would attach great importance to being able to catch them, and feel they have more angling skill if they catch a lot. What these small waters do is provide entertainment in catching trout. Even some fishery owners agree with this, but they are in business to sell trout fishing, and if the angler wants to believe it is his skill that caught him the fish, then that's fine by the owner. A happy customer should come back.

Small waters are now an integral part of our trout fishing scene—in fact I would even say they have taken over from true trout fishing. The demand for instant fish is there, and will continue to be there, as long as fishermen want easy fishing. I would suggest though that you do not worry too much about the type of angler who thinks he is better than you just because he goes to the small waters so much he knows the routine of the fish.

I shall now let you in on the routine, with a few tips that will catch you more trout. But don't think I'm skilful. I have merely adapted to the way of extracting trout from these entertainment venues in the most interesting ways possible. First, trout stocked the night before will always come to the fly better than those stocked in the morning, before opening. They have more time to settle down to their new environment, and of course they will be getting hungry.

Most day ticket waters that produce a lot of fish have to stock on a daily basis. To do this they need a Land Rover or truck with a tank on the back. They aren't going to put a couple of trout in here, a couple there, a few over by the weedbed. They want to get the fish in the water fast, so that none die. Therefore they will probably tip them in at the easiest access point for the Land Rover or truck. In fact at a lot of fisheries you will see at either end of the lakes the deep ruts where the water has slopped out of the tank, softening the earth, and the daily routine has seen the weight of the truck bed the ground down. That's the easiest way to locate a good starting point. I would be most surprised if you didn't get a take from a fish in the first six casts. Even if you don't see any ruts or track marks, go to the end of the lake with the deepest water. These are often good stock fish holding areas and well worth starting at. The best places of all on the small waters are those with a bay or lagoon with a depth of three to six feet. This corresponds with the size and depth of most trout stew ponds, and very often these stock fish stay where they have been put simply because of the association with home.

A second tip, and one I have not seen elsewhere, is that most trout in a stew pond swim in a set direction if the pond has anything like a circular shape. They do this all their lives. When they are stocked, providing they find an area of lake that bears some similarity to the stew pond, they will settle down and work round in a circle, just as they did before. I have heard 'experts' say that the biggest rainbows settle down to 'patrol' on a set route. They don't 'patrol', it's just that they have been held in a stew pond for longer than a 2-lb trout, and are therefore much more conditioned to swimming on a set route. There is no territorial instinct in this, in fact I have seen a 2-lb fish chase off a ten-pounder! But this information can be used to good effect if you find a bay or inlet.

If you don't present the fly to a cruising fish correctly, don't thrash the water to a foam in an effort to reach him. Never outstretch what you know to be your normal distance, not so much because you may frighten the fish, but because he is going to come round in a circle

Feeding times should be observed if the fishery has its own stewponds. Being fed several times a day, the trout, when stocked into a lake, will be at its most vulnerable at those times.

again, and so give you plenty of time to take your shot and make it count. If there is a group of fish, and I've seen anything from four to twenty milling around in the corner of a lake, then you can take advantage of their competition to get a violent greedy take.

76

You can use this advantage if you have other anglers who have already cast at the same fish. Cast out as normal, but as the leader commences its arc of unrolling, pull down with your left hand as though you were stripping line in. It might also pay you to cast a little harder to speed up the weighted nymph. This in effect punches the nymph hard through the surface film, and creates quite a 'blip' on the surface. The trout will have been stocked the previous night or that morning, and will be well tuned in to what a 'blip' on the surface means. They will think you've come to feed them from the dustbin of pellets, and race over to gobble up the nearest thing. There's no skill in this, it's merely that I'm using the extreme conditioning of those fish to create an advantage over both them and the other anglers, who after all are competitors for those same fish. I have seen people cast at a group of trout, have seen one break off and follow the fly, and have 'blipped' my leaded nymph down hard enough on the surface to actually make them break off from the first fly, and race over to grab mine! The other anglers didn't realise this had happened, and believed I had hooked another fish in the group.

Another tip I've yet to read about is that the bigger the trout is, the more conditioned he is, and therefore the more gullible he should be. Sometimes a trout gets pricked and lost, or broken off by an angler. Such a fish has learned something and he represents more of a challenge next time round. There's usually a big fish in every lake, everybody knows about it, but nobody can get it to look at anything. It probably means that several people thrashed flies at it early on in the day, thoroughly upsetting it, and sending it charging around the lake, making some anglers think it is feeding on minnows. By lunchtime the anglers have tired, caught their limit, or generally given the fish up as uncatchable. There aren't many fish that are uncatchable, it's merely that the restriction on techniques and methods make it difficult.

If you have taken any time to talk to the fishery owner you might have gleaned some information as to the exact times he feeds the various grades of fish in the stock ponds. You can find out exactly what times he feeds the 1–3-lb fish, the 4–8-lb fish, and most important, the 10–15-lb fish. By finding out these times and jotting them down, you can allocate yourself a period of the day when a big fish is most likely to respond to something in the water. By afternoon nearly all the fish not caught are tired from being thoroughly frightened, pricked or broken off, and will be settling down to a slow cruise, or even be stationary in the water. If the fish between 10 and 15 lb are fed at 9 am, 12 pm and 4 pm, the two times you want to try throwing leaded nymphs at them are about 12.10 and 4.10. It's no good in the morning, because there will be too many anglers about to upset them. By lunchtime a lot of the anglers will have disappeared, and within as little as half an hour those fish will have settled down. Even if you spot the big one earlier, don't panic. You are much more likely to get a response at those feeding times than any other. And of course the confinement conditioning of the fish will mean he will come round in that area sooner or later.

One of the basic problems in catching big trout, over say 5 lbs, is that the angler simply isn't getting his nymph down to that trout's area. Big fish are fed on quite chunky pellets, and you should try to aim for a nymph size comparable, or slightly larger than the pellet. Big fish will rarely tip up and suck down a dry fly off the surface. They want some 'meat and potatoes' so give them this in the shape of a chunky, heavily leaded nymph. Standard wet flies just don't get down to them quickly enough. It's fine if you are pulling the fly back blind, using a sinking line, but your chances of the fly passing within six inches of the trout's nose are remote to say the least. You may by sheer chance be pulling through at the depth he is swimming at, but you have no way of knowing where he is. The best way to convince yourself of this is to throw a long fast sink line out into the middle of the lake. After three pulls you will see the biggest trout of your life cruising past about three feet from the bank edge! You just can't aerialise 30 yards of fast sink line in one movement. So try to walk round, without any blind casting, until you see the big fish, which will probably be quite close in anyway. Then cast well ahead of him, at least six feet, and let the leader and fly get down quickly to where you judge his depth to be. Remember in clear waters he is going to be a lot deeper than he appears. When the trout and estimated fly position are about a foot apart, strip in sharply a couple of times and judge his reaction. He may turn upwards or to the side without taking, but this will at least let you know you were incorrect with your fly placement.

Fly Fishing

While small waters need to stock every day in order to maintain fish density, the larger reservoirs stock smaller fish but in greater numbers. These are still not true wild fish but as they have to grow naturally in larger, open waters, they are as near to true wild fish as we can get. The author believes it is from these small trout that our reservoirs may hold monster Browns. With a diet of the small fingerling stock fish, the scenario becomes similar to that of Utah's Flaming Gorge Reservoir where the big lake Brown and Rainbow trout eat these same stockfish to reach over and above the 30/40 lb range.

Next time cast further ahead and wait a bit longer. Sometimes you can actually see the trout open its mouth and close it over the fly. An upward lift of the rod will set the hook. If you get only a couple of responses from the trout, or if he is in slightly murky water where you cannot actually see the fly, watch his mouth. If you know the fly and trout are in close proximity and can see his big white mouth open and close further than usual, then hit him. It's a gamble that has often paid off.

They will sometimes make two mouthing movements. The first is when it sucks the fly in, the second is when it doesn't like the taste of fur and feather, and spits it out. Don't bother striking if you see the second movement, it's too late and you may alarm him even more. You must strike on that first movement or not at all.

Another method to use if the trout looks a bit uninterested is to cast out and let the fly sit on the bottom. When he comes round, let him get about three feet from it then tweak it back off the bottom a couple of times. If you send up puffs of mud or weed, so much the better because this will attract him. Again, watch his reaction, and don't take your eyes off his mouth movements.

Sometimes even this doesn't work, and you must conceal yourself even further. This is generally the case where the trout's association with man has changed completely. When first stocked he is a complete dummy, and if you present a big nymph to him correctly, he is yours. However after a week or so of constant attention from anglers he will have a healthy respect for anglers waving rods. Position yourself where you know he is liable to show at some time and put a weedbed between you and the fish. As soon as he appears lay out a fly across the end of the weedbed in the clear water where you know he will pass. When fly and trout are in close proximity, commence the retrieve, and see what response you get. Don't forget to watch those mouth movements. First bite he's yours, second bite the fly is back in the water.

One of the best tips I can give any angler stalking any size of fish in a small water, is to show him the fly first, not the leader. Assuming you have taken two or three 'dummy' stock fish, you may be struggling to complete your quota. Contrary to the old school of thought that you must always approach a trout from behind, I am

The close observation of feeding patterns has rewarded the author with many big trout like this Rainbow. He attributes such captures not to angling skill but purely to acquired knowledge; learning to do something the anglers around him haven't yet thought of.

going to suggest that you cast a fly directly at a trout that is approaching you. If you can't do this, alter your positioning carefully, so you have a fish coming as near directly at you as possible. Cast about six feet in front of him, then when the fish is about two feet from the fly, start taking it away from him. The response is nearly always immediate. Even if he doesn't engulf your fly, half the leader and maybe the rod, he will charge after it, often turning away at the last minute. You have made him respond where previously he wouldn't even increase cruising speed. That's because previously he had seen the leader sinking as well as the fly. By keeping him coming directly at you, the fly is the only part nearest to him.

Go Fishing for Trout

Many of the small waters are quite shallow and being spring fed in one way or another are subject to intensive sunlight. This in turn creates weed and algal blooms that can either colour the whole of the water from top to bottom, or the top six inches, or grow in mats on the bottom. Some of this is like what is known as blanket weed, which grows green on the bottom of the lake bed, and dies off and floats to the surface during the hot months. When it gets to this stage it is subject to any wind drift, and can be blown into one area of bank in a tight mat. Don't neglect these areas, for they invariably house plenty of fish.

In bright weather, once the few remaining stockfish have recovered from the criss-crossing of fly lines, and the anglers have worn themselves out casting, the fish retire into the shade of these weed blankets. There are two ways to winkle them out. One is to fish a floating line with a fast sink braided Airflo leader. Make your cast slightly upwind and across the front edge of the weed mat, and let the wind drift the fly line near the edge. Retrieve in sharp jerks with a pause in between and you should get a response.

The other way is to stand right where the floating weed mat is thickest. You can either scoop a hole in it with your net, which might frighten the fish, and colour the water, or poke your rod top through it to make a small hole, just large enough to lower your fly through. This sounds unusual, but is in fact standard summer practice at many waters. Lower your fly through, using a weighted nymph with a very accentuated breather hackle. Let it go down a few feet, then jig it up and down in two-inch movements to make the breather hackle pulsate. Don't be surprised when your rod top gets wrenched under the weed, there is in fact little need to strike. Put your tippet strength up to at least 6 lb, as you are going to have to hit the fish and hold it, getting it in the net in the shortest time possible. If it gets your leader wrapped up in the weed mat it will snap it like cotton, even on 4-lb tippet.

In clear water, with a big fish, say over 5 lb, the only advice on fighting techniques I can give is to take line at your earliest convenience. These bigger trout are conditioned to being netted out, so you aren't likely to get an epic two-hour battle out of them. Most fish over 10 lb flop their way into the net, providing you have the courage to hold them hard enough. All they do is thrash the water to a foam in a sideways movement of the body. It doesn't occur to them to turn round and bolt away from you. Can you imagine hooking a 12-lb wild steelhead trout in a big Alaskan river, then trying to 'flop' him into your net?

Stew pond rainbows and wild rainbows are the same fish scientifically, but very different on the hook! You have two methods of fighting a fish. You can either strip line in with your retrieve hand, or wind all the slack up and then play him from the reel. This at least allows you to follow the fish, but as you are hardly going to walk more than a few paces with them, I would advise playing them by stripping in the line. I have a friend from Essex, who persists in letting a load of slack develop when he has hooked a fish, just so that he can play the fish on the reel. He likes the pretty clicking sound, but I have seen him lose at least twenty good trout over the years while he 'plays with the clicking sound'! The moral is, if you can get line then take it.

I recently wrote a guide round the small waters in the south of England. During the research for the book I confirmed what I had already thought for years—that there are only a few flies you need to take these stocked trout. The flies that most fishery owners advised me to use, were all similar, even though their fishery might not have had a good hatch of the natural insect. Try these to start with: Mayfly Nymph, Montana Nymph, Damsel Nymph, Teleco Nymph, Corixa, Pheasant Tail Nymph, Gold Ribbed Hare's Ear, Black Aggravator, Lime Green Baby Doll (tied leaded and stubby on a size 10 hook), Stickfly, Muddler Minnow, Viva, Appetiser, Green Beast, Black Buzzer, Jack Frost, and Lead Bug. My most successful models are the Lime Green Baby Doll, and the Black Aggravator (my own fly). But the best without a doubt is the Lead Bug. This is so easy most people don't believe it catches fish. It is a variation of the Oliver Kite Bare Hook Nymph, which was quite simply a bare hook with turns of copper wire round the shank.

However, the Lead Bug was not born of such class. There are several people who go round the fisheries and foul hook their fish. Brook trout were the classic example. These were a cold-water species of trout, so when they started to be stocked in our summer warmed lakes they simply remained stationary in the water. They also had white leading edges to their pectoral, ventral and anal fins, which meant they were a sitting target to the snatchers, or foul hooking brigade. It soon started being used at big fish waters like Avington, and one young man took a string of big rainbows and browns over a season by snatching them using a treble hook with lead wire wrapped round the shank. He even had a selection of different weighted 'rippers' in his wallet. After a while everyone became suspicious about these incredible catches and they were forced to use the hooks in holes in the weed. While trying to snatch trout they discovered that those they missed actually whipped round and grabbed the jiggling trebles. Thus the Lead Bug was born, albeit out of a dubious past. Quite why the trout take it nobody knows, but they certainly do.

There is a bit of an art to fishing then. You need a floating line and, a short leader of about nine feet, degreasing the leader over its entire length. You cast out, the bug drops down the length of the leader in about three seconds, then you strip it back in really violent three-inch jerks. The crash takes you get are amazing, and they work even better if you spot a fish lying on its own, that's refused every fly thrown at it. Cast the Lead Bug out, give it a second, then keeping the rod high, jiggle it up and down using the rod top, making the bug rise and fall rapidly in three-inch movements. This works best close in, when the trout are no more than twenty feet out. You can see them go crazy to get it. I can only assume the trout get used to the horizontal or slowly rising motion of the standard retrieve, then they suddenly see this hairless thing flashing up and down in a vertical motion. Another top fly angler told me it might be because it looks like a giant hatching buzzer. The weight of the lead makes the hookshank hang vertically, and the hook bend making it look like a buzzer. Personally I think it's the violent jiggling action. Give it a try, it's so good it could well be banned!

World Records for Line Class and Fly-Rod Catches

Line Class	2 lb	4 lb	8 lb	12 lb	16 lb	20 lb	30 lb	50 lb	80 lb
Trout brook	7 lb 8 oz	8 lb 4 oz	8 lb 4 oz	6 lb 4 oz	5 lb 14 oz	4 lb 3 oz			
Tippet (fly-rod)	8 lb 4 oz	10 lb	10 lb 7 oz	9 lb 4 oz	9 lb 2 oz				
Trout brown	16 lb	27 lb 9 oz	33 lb 8 oz	34 lb 6 oz	21 lb 5 oz	24 lb 12 oz	17 lb 10 oz	14 lb 4 oz	
Tippet	10 lb 9 oz	12 lb 3 oz	27 lb 3 oz	12 lb	4 lb 11 oz				
Trout bull	6 lb 4 oz	7 lb 7 oz	12 lb 4 oz	17 lb 11 oz	19 lb 6 oz	*13 lb 4 oz			
Tippet	4 lb	4 lb 12 oz	2 lb 4 oz	0.00	0.00				
Trout cutthroat	9 lb 14 oz	10 lb 14 oz	13 lb 8 oz	11 lb 12 oz	11 lb 12 oz	11 lb 6 oz			
Tippet	8 lb 9 oz	5 lb 15 oz	14 lb 1 oz	0.00	0.00				
Trout golden	3 lb 13 oz	1 lb 8 oz	2 lb	2 lb 11 oz	0.00				
Tippet	1 lb 11 oz	1 lb 2 oz	1 lb	0.00					
Trout lake	28 lb 5 oz	31 lb 8 oz	38 lb	50 lb 8 oz	53 lb 4 oz	63 lb 9 oz	60 lb 12 oz	50 lb	34 lb 1 oz
Tippet	13 lb 8 oz	17 lb 8 oz	20 lb 10 oz	17 lb 7 oz	9 lb				
Trout rainbow	18 lb 4 oz	23 lb 12 oz	26 lb 9 oz	29 lb 1 oz	30 lb 9 oz	31 lb 5 oz	30 lb 5 oz	19 lb 14 oz	
Tippet	16 lb 8 oz	19 lb 13 oz	24 lb 8 oz	22 lb 8 oz	28 lb				
Trout tiger	0.00	4 lb 3 oz	11 lb 9 oz	0.00	0.00	20 lb 13 oz	0.00		
Tippet	0.00	0.00	0.00	0.00	0.00				

* Records which have been tied

85

There are many ways to eat a trout but possibly the richest flavour is obtained by smoking. Here Peter Atkinson hangs a rack of small trout in one of his smoke houses for curing. He does all the work himself, right down to packaging and marketing to ensure the best quality product.

The Art of Smoking

We are all familiar with the strong taste of smoked trout, and have doubtless seen it on a restaurant menu, but how is is done? Could you do it with any fish or meat? What is the correct way to smoke a trout? To answer these queries, and give trout anglers an idea of what it entails, I contacted Peter Atkinson, formerly a trout fishery manager, now the owner of Atkinson Smoked Foods at Exton near Southampton. As a fishery manager Peter had to deal with the constant demand of anglers, asking him where they could get their catch smoked. He decided to investigate, and after initial successes at his fishery, he expanded into building his own smokery. There was no way he could compete with the giant supermarket chains, but he didn't want to. What he aimed for was a traditionally smoked fish, done entirely by him from gutting, right through to delivering it to chosen food outlets in special vacuum-sealed packs.

I took an evening's drive down through the beautiful Meon valley to interview Peter, and his knowledge on the subject may be of interest to fishermen. Traditional smoking means not using modern electrical equipment, thermostatically controlled and geared to mass production. By getting back to the basics of the trade he could offer his clients a wider variety of flavours. The secret with his method is to keep a constant temperature at all times. He began by making his own kilns at home.

One of the largest areas where traditional smoking is still done is Scotland. This was largely due to the salmon fishing industry, and in Scotland there were smoke houses as large as barns. It should be remembered that smoking was used as a method of preservation before the age of refrigeration. The Scots started using oak simply because of its availability. In trying to follow their methods, Peter had difficulty initially in securing a good supply of oak sawdust for burning. You have to have the right grade of chips, using hardwoods only, as softwood give the fish a different flavour and can even make it taste sour. The kiln can develop a build-up of tar from the sap of the softwoods, which can taint the food.

Peter much prefers oak, although he has used beech, ash and elm, which are all hardwoods. Traditional smokers can also create their very own flavour. Some people burn gorse bushes or dried leaves as flavour enhancers, or to give the meat an aromatic flavour.

There are two methods of smoking, cold and hot. Cold smoking is a method Peter uses for trout in excess of 3 lb, which of course is a lot less by the time it is gutted, trimmed and smoked. He guts first, even down to removing the gills, but leaving in the gill bone, which he uses as a 'handle' to hang the fish in the smoker with. Some processes lay the fish flat, but this method entails hanging the fish vertically so that the oil can drain out properly. The smoke gets all round the hung fish, whereas if they are racked flat, those on the lower rack have to be moved higher during the full smoking process. Trout up to 2 lb are opened out and split, after which he will smoke just the fillet itself. The backbone is removed, but the ribs are left in as supports for the flesh. Then the trout is salted or brined. Salting is the method he favours. A fresh fish is salted on a basis of one hour per pound, the salt having the effect of removing any excess moisture from the flesh.

With cold smoking, the trout is not really cooked by heat, but is preserved by dehydration. Once the salt has been washed off, the trout is hung up by the gill bone to dry for a while, then placed in the cold smoker. Depending on the size of the fish this can take up to 24 hours, with big salmon or jumbo trout taking from 36 hours to two days. The cold smoker must be used in conjunction with the temperature outside, and will work more quickly in summer, and more slowly in December, depending on the external temperature. This is where an electronic unit comes into its own in the commercial field, as being thermostatically controlled, it can be adjusted to take into account the ambient temperatures at different times of year. Too

The Art of Smoking

As well as smoking trout, Peter Atkinson prides himself on providing a service that can give you a sliced and replaced whole fish – trout or salmon – fit for a banquet.

high a humidity level will prevent this dehydrating process. You can tell when the fish is done, according to Peter, when the skin dries on its back. During the last hour of smoking he may raise the temperature to finalise the back skin drying. The meat should take on a golden hue, with a glossy effect as the oil comes out. Temperature ranges for cold smoking are between 70° and 80 °F, so on a hot summer day it can be difficult to prevent the temperature climbing too high. Contrary to popular belief, the wood must smoulder and smoke, not flare up. It is the smoke which flavours it, not the heat from the burning oak dust.

After the smoking has finished, the trout is taken out, the gill bone, pectoral and ribs are removed, as well as a 'skirt' of excess fat along the belly, which is trimmed off level. The 'pin' bones are then removed and the smoked trout is ready to eat as a complete fillet. Some people want to see it sliced, and to cater for the discerning gourmet, Peter has a slicing machine with a circular blade designed for skinning carcasses at an abbatoir, that cuts the fillet into wafer-thin slices. He can actually slice a complete fillet, remove it from the skin, then lay each slice back in its original position with a thin piece of cellophane between each slice for presentation.

The hot smoking process is only used for the smaller fish, generally under 1 lb, that can be smoked as a whole fish. These small fish don't break up. If you hot smoke a whole large fish, you are actually cooking it by heat, and the flesh starts to break up, and falls in the fire. To prepare for the hot smoker, Peter prefers a brine solution, immersing the fish for a shorter period, using an 80 per cent saturation solution, with 2 lb 10$^3/_4$ oz of vacuum-dried salt, to a gallon of water. There are also specific brining salts complete with additives than can be used, but as traditional smoking is his hallmark, so he likes to keep to the manual methods. A $^3/_4$-lb trout gets brined for one hour, then cold smoked for twelve hours. From here it is placed in the hot smoker with a big oak fire set at 200 °F, finishing in the last half hour at 220 °F. It only takes four hours at this heat. It is of course not direct heat from the flames, but heat from the smoke that does the cooking. The first sign that the trout is done is when the skin crinkles, and it is confirmed when you can squeeze excess oil out near the tail. There is also a weight loss of between 30 and 40 per cent because of dehydration. With cold smoking you can get up to 50 per cent weight loss.

Aiming for the traditional flavour, Peter uses no additives at all. Some of the older smokers use juniper berries in the oak powder to achieve a different flavour, and things like molasses, or various spirits like whisky, brandy or rum (which is highly popular) will add flavour. Peter, however, believes the flavour is better maintained by perfect curing and smoking than by the inclusion of any additive.

As for the kilns in which the smoking is done, a bigger space is better for cold smoking because of the dispersal of the smoke, and at the moment his premises are being changed to a remote fire pit. This means the actual fire burns away from the chamber, and the smoke is drawn through the fish by convection through pipes. The same principle is used for the hot smoker, but the chamber is much smaller, although the fire is bigger to achieve the heat range required. You can even get electrically heated kilns or hot air fans, but Peter feels you cannot beat the flavour of his fish.

He can also do meats, poultry, game, venison, and wants to try quails. Some people think that hanging game such as pheasants is the same as smoking, because the flavour is strong. This is not so, however, and the flavour of oak smoke is unlike any other. For smoking bacon he uses a salt and sugar cure, rubbed into the meat over 3–5 days until the raw pork side turns green. Then the solution is washed off, and the meat is cold smoked for up to three days prior to vacuum packing. Even then, the meat must be properly cooked before eating.

Some smoked flavours are not truly smoked, but are merely additives put on the product to create a similar flavour.

Peter was proud to say he smoked the first ever double-figure triploid rainbow which came from Nythe Lake. He said it came out terrible because being a sterile fish its main object in life was to eat, and it therefore had too high a fat content, and no muscle tissue. The largest fish he has so far smoked are a salmon of 35 lb and a rainbow of 16 lb.

It's a common belief among game fishermen, that you only send the older, rough-looking fish to the smokers, fish that are too poor in quality to eat fresh. Peter believes that if a fish is in poor condition in the first place it will stay that way even when smoked. Brown trout taste just as good after smoking as rainbow, and there is no one strain of rainbow that smokes any differently, or tastes any better than others.

Another fallacy is that rainbows with the pinkest flesh taste the best. This was said to be due to their diet of shrimps in the wild, but it transpires that the colour is fed to them by the trout farm, in the form of a pigmentation in the pellets! If a rainbow is fed on unpigmented pellets its flesh will be white, and it will taste just the same as a trout with pink flesh!

Of course there are those of you who still like their trout lightly grilled with a lemon squeeze, knob of butter and sprig of parsley. But once you've tasted one of Peter Atkinson's traditional smoked trout, there should be no doubt left in your mind as to which has the better flavour.

Facing page: A guide to Partridge Trout and Grayling Fly Hooks. Hooks not to size.

Appendix

A–Albert Partridge Wide Gape Down Eye Hooks

For standard and soft hackle wet flies; short bodied nymphs; and very strong dry flies with down eye. An offset bend – middle weight wire.

AFY–Barbless Wide Gape Down Eye Hooks

Identical with Code A hooks except they are barbless and with flat (not offset) bend. Sizes 10, 12 and 14

B–Albert Partridge Wide Gape Up Eye Hooks

For strong dry flies with an up eye. Identical with Code A except for an up eye.

D3ST–Straight Eye Streamer Hooks (originally known as "Partridge Lure Hooks")

For lures, streamers, bucktails, muddlers and any fly on a long shank hook with a straight eye, e.g. longer nymphs.

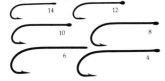

D4A–Bucktail/Streamer Hooks

For lures, bucktails, streamers, muddlers and longer nymphs on a graceful down eye hook.

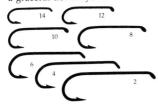

D4AY–Barbless Bucktail/Streamer Hooks

Identical with Code D4A except these are barbless. Sizes 8 and 10

D5B–Mayfly Hooks

E1A–Hooper L/S Dry Fly Hooks (Down Eye)

For slightly longer dry flies and floating nymph patterns. A 4 × fine hook with about 1 × long shank and down eye.

E3AY–Barbless Hooper L/S Dry Fly Hooks (Down Eye)

Identical with E1A but barbless. Sizes 10, 12, 14, 16, 18

E6A–Hooper 1 × Short Dry Fly Hooks (Down Eye)

For standard and lightly dressed dry flies of all kinds. Slightly shorter than standard, 4 × fine hook with down eye.

G3A–Sproat Forged Wet Fly Hooks

For wet flies and heavier nymphs. Sproat style but forged bend for great strength.

H1A–Captain Hamilton Nymph Hooks

For longer nymphs, lightweight lures and streamer flies. Captain Hamilton wide gape and about 2½ × long on middleweight wire.

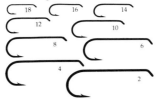

H3ST–Draper Flat Bodied Nymph Hooks

For imitations of all flat wide bodied nymphs. Unique design with serrated shanks for easier tying.

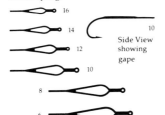

Side View showing gape

J1A–Partridge Limerick Wet Fly Hooks

For traditional wet flies. Heavyweight wire – very strong.

K1A–Vince Marinaro Midge Hooks

For tiny midge and caenis dry flies and midge pupa. Offset bend to aid hooking and slightly turned down eye.

K2B–Yorkshire Sedge Hooks

For sedge pupa and larva, shrimp and grub patterns, and "upside down" flies. Slight up eye aids hooking and fine curved shank.

K3A–Swedish Dry Fly Hooks

For sedge and longer dry flies usually tied upside down. (Tying instructions sheet available from Partridge).

K4A–John Veniard Grub/Shrimp Hooks

For grub and shrimp imitations curved body nymphs and some dry flies. Offset bend with curved shank.

K12ST–Long Shank Sedge Hooks

For sedge larva and pupa, shrimp, dragon fly nymphs, buzzers and most emerger patterns.

L2A–Captain Hamilton Wet Fly Hooks

For lighter wet flies and nymphs and strong dry flies with down eye.

L3A–Captain Hamilton Dry Fly Hooks (Down Eye)

For all kinds of dry flies.
4 × fine lightweight wire.

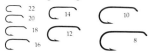

L3AY–Barbless Captain Hamilton Dry Fly Hooks (Down Eye)

Identical with L3A but barbless.
Sizes 10, 12, 14, 16, 18

L3B–Captain Hamilton Dry Fly Hooks (Up Eye)

Identical with L3A but an up eye.

L4A–Captain Hamilton Featherweight Dry Fly Hooks

For no hackle very lightly dressed dry flies and floating nymphs.
6 × fine wire and down eye.

R1A–Double Limerick Hooks

Identical with J1A but a double version and therefore slightly shorter in body length.
For traditional wet flies and point flies. A really strong hook.

Sizes 2, 4, 6, 8, 10, 12

R2A – Outpoint Double Hooks

For small wet flies, modelled on Loch Leven doubles.

CS2 BL S.E.B. X Strong Lure Hooks (Black)

For heavy lures and big fish. Based on salmon hook design with looped down eye – Black finish.

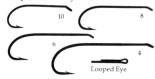

Looped Eye

CS2 SI S.E.B. X Strong Lure Hooks (Silver)

As CS2 BL but silver. Sizes 4, 6, 8, 10

CS7–Captain Hamilton International Series of Hooks

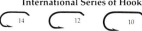

CS7SHW–Superheavyweight

For heavy wet flies and nymphs.

CS7HW–Heavyweight

For standard wet flies and nymphs.

CS7MW–Middleweight

For lighter wet flies and nymphs.

Size 10 hooks of each weight are made to conform to "International" and "Benson and Hedges" maximum permissible size.
Extra wide gape and black finish.

CS11–J.S. Stainless Steel Sea Streamer Hooks

For streamer flies used in salt or brackish water or lures with silver bodies. Modelled on D4A hooks but non-rusting stainless steel and therefore silver finish.

CS20–Roman Moser Arrowpoint (Barbless) Dry Fly Hooks

For all types of dry flies and floating nymphs. Unique barbless arrowpoint hooks which hold just as well as barbed hooks. Otherwise modelled on E6A design.

Arrow Point

GREYSHADOW SERIES

Flashpointed with "Niflor" finish

GRS 2A–Captain Hamilton Wet Fly Hooks

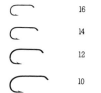

GRS 3A–Captain Hamilton Dry Fly Hooks

GRS 4A–Bucktail/Streamer Hooks

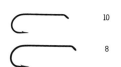

GRS 12ST–Emerger/Nymph Hooks

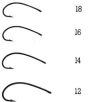

GO FISHING FOR

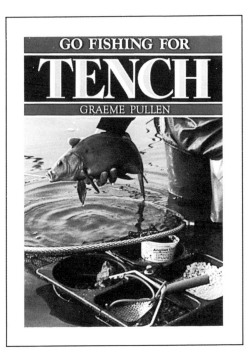

All available in the same series at £9.95 each.

96pp, 240 x 172mm
16pp colour and approx. 30 black & white photographs.